Skye & Outer Hebrides

Alan Murphy

D1205394

Credits

Footprint credits

Editor: Alan Murphy
Production and layout: Angus Dawson,
Emma Bryers
Maps: Kevin Feeney

Managing Director: Andy Riddle
Commercial Director: Patrick Dawson
Publisher: Alan Murphy
Publishing Managers: Felicity Laughton,
Nicola Gibbs.
Digital Editors: Jo Williams,
Tom Mellors
Marketing and PR: Liz Harper
Sales: Diane McEntee
Advertising: Renu Sibal
Finance and Administration:
Elizabeth Taylor

Photography credits
Front cover: Joe Gough/Shutterstock
Back cover: Trotternish, Karola i Marek/
Shutterstock

Printed in Great Britain by CPI Antony Rowe,
Chippenham, Wiltshire

Every effort has been made to ensure that
the facts in this guidebook are accurate.
However, travellers should still obtain advice
from consulates, airlines, etc about travel
and visa requirements before travelling.
The authors and publishers cannot
accept responsibility for any loss, injury or
inconvenience however caused.

Publishing information
Footprint *Focus Skye & Outer Hebrides*
1st edition
© Footprint Handbooks Ltd
July 2011

ISBN: 978 1 908206 06 0
CIP DATA: A catalogue record for this book is
available from the British Library

® Footprint Handbooks and the Footprint
mark are a registered trademark of Footprint
Handbooks Ltd

Published by Footprint
6 Riverside Court
Lower Bristol Road
Bath BA2 3DZ, UK
T +44 (0)1225 469141
F +44 (0)1225 469461
footprinttravelguides.com

Distributed in the USA by Globe Pequot
Press, Guilford, Connecticut

The content of Footprint *Focus Skye & Outer
Hebrides* has been taken directly from
Footprint's *Scotland Highlands &
Islands Handbook* which was researched
and written by Alan Murphy.

Contents

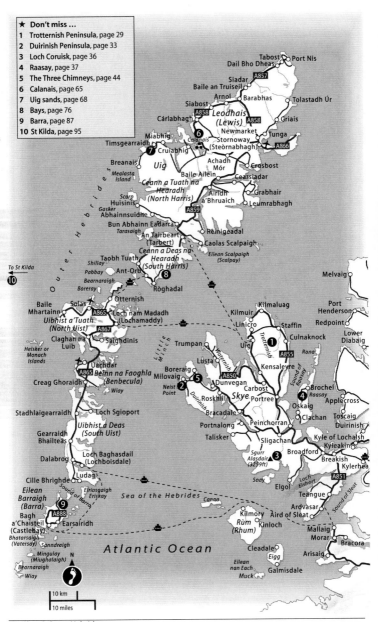

★ Don't miss ...

To St Kilda

Tabost
Port Nis
Dail Bho Dheas
Siadar
Baile an Truiseil
Arnol
Barabhas
Tolastadh Úr
Siabost
A858
Leodhais
(Lewis)
A858
Griais
Càrlabhag
Newmarket
A866
Miabhig
Calanais
Stornoway
(Steòrnabhagh)
Timsgearraidh
Cruiabhig
Achadh
Mór
Crosbost
Breanais
Baile Ailein
Cearstadar
Mealasta
island
Uig
Grabhair
Ceann a Tuath na
Hearadh
(North Harris)
Airidh
a'Bhruaich
Leumrabhagh
Scarp
Huisinis
Gasker
Abhainnsuidhe
Rèinigeadal
Tarasaigh
Bun Abhainn Eadarra
An Tairbeart
(Tarbert)
Caolas Scalpaigh
Eilean Scalpaigh
(Scalpay)
Ceann a Deas na
Hearadh
(South Harris)
Melvaig
Shillay
Taobh Tuath
Pabbay
Ant-Ob
Bearnaraigh
Boreray
Ròghadal
Baile
Mhartainn
Solas
Otternish
Kilmaluag
Port
Henderson
Uibhist a'Tuath
(North Uist)
A865
Loch nam Madadh
(Lochamaddy)
A867
Kilmuir
Kilmuir
Staffin
Redpoint
Claghan na
Luib
Saighdinis
Linicro
Uig
Lower
Diabaig
Heisker or
Monach
Islands
Uachdar
Trumpan
Uig
Trotternish
A855
Rona
Creag Ghoraidh
Beinn na Faoghla
(Benbecula)
Lusta
Boreraig
Milovaig
Neist
Point
The Three Chimneys
Dunvegan
Carbost
Kensaleyre
Portree
Brochel
Raasay
Applecross
Wiay
Roskhill
Skye
Clachan
Toscaig
Stadhlaigearraidh
Loch Sgioport
Bracadale
Peinchorran
Duirinish
Gearraidh
Bhailteas
Uibhist a Deas
(South Uist)
Portnalong
Sligachan
Kyle of Lochalsh
Kyleakin
Talisker
Sgurr
Alasdair
(3259ft)
Breakish
Dalabrog
Loch Baghasdail
(Lochboisdale)
Broadford
Kylerhea
Ludag
Elgol
Soay
Loch
Eishort
A851
Cille Bhrighde
Eriosgaigh
Eriskay
Sea of the Hebrides
Canaa
Teangue
Eilean
Barraigh
(Barra)
Kilmory
Rùm
(Rhum)
Àird of Sleat
Ardvasar
Bagh
a'Chaisteil
(Castlebay)
Earsairidh
Kinloch
Mallaig
Morar
Bhatarsaigh
(Vatersay)
Sanndraigh
Cleadale
Eigg
Bracora
Mingulay
(Miughalaigh)
Eilean
nan Each
Muck
Galmisdale
Arisaig
Bearnaraigh
Wiay
Atlantic Ocean

N

10 km
10 miles

The Isle of Skye (An t-Eilean Sgitheanach) is the best known of all the Scottish islands. The island's spectacular combination of mountains and sea creates some of Britain's most breathtaking scenery. Standing in the centre of the island are the Cuillins. These proud, implacable mountains are the greatest concentration of peaks in Britain and among the most challenging. The Small Isles is the collective name given to the four islands of Eigg, Muck, Rùm and Canna, lying south of Skye. Seen from the mainland, they look a very tempting prospect, especially the jagged outline of Rùm and curiously shaped Eigg that's now owned by its tiny community. The determined traveller, with time on their hands, will be well rewarded, particularly on Eigg and mountainous Rùm, with its superb walking and abundant wildlife.

The Outer Hebrides are a narrow, 130-mile-long chain of more than 200 islands lying 40 miles off the northwest coast of the Scottish mainland. Despite the frequency of transport connections with the mainland, the Outer Hebrides remain remote in every sense. Unlike Skye and the Inner Hebrides, tourism is of far less importance to the local economy. In many ways, the islands are the last bastion of the old Highland life. Though newer industries such as fish farming have been introduced, the traditional occupations of crofting, fishing and weaving still dominate and, outside Stornoway, life is very much a traditional one, revolving around the seasons and the tides. Relentlessly battered by fierce Atlantic winds, the islands can seem a hostile environment and an unappealing proposition. Much of the interior is bleak peat bog, rocks and endless tiny lochs, and the long, straggling crofting communities only add to the feeling of desolation. But anyone who has stood on a clifftop and felt a thrill at the power and potential of all that water should come here. Nowhere else in Britain is there such a sense of emptiness and of the sheer forces of nature.

Planning your trip

Getting there

Air

Generally speaking, the cheapest and quickest way to travel to Scotland from outside the UK is by air. There are good links to Edinburgh and Glasgow, with direct flights from many European cities, and direct flights from North America to Glasgow. There are also flights from a few European cities to Aberdeen and Inverness. There are no direct flights from North America to Edinburgh; these are usually routed via London or Dublin. There are also daily flights from Ireland and regular flights to most Scottish airports from other parts of the UK. There are no direct flights to Scotland from Australia, New Zealand, South Africa or Japan; you will have to get a connection from London.

From the UK and Ireland There are direct flights to Scotland's four main airports – Glasgow, Edinburgh, Aberdeen and Inverness – almost hourly from London Heathrow, Gatwick, Stansted and Luton airports. There are also daily flights from provincial UK airports and from Dublin. To fly on to the smaller airports, you'll need to change planes, see page 9, for domestic flights. The cheapest flights leave from London Luton or Stansted, plus a few provincial airports, with **Ryanair** and **easyJet**. If you book online, fares can be as little as £5 one-way during promotions (excluding taxes), but usually you can expect to fly for under £70 return if you can be flexible with dates and times. These tickets are often subject to rigid restrictions, but the savings can make the extra effort worthwhile. Cheaper tickets usually have to be bought at least a week in advance and apply to only a few midweek flights. They are also non-refundable, or only partly refundable, and non-transferable. A standard flexible and refundable fare from London to Glasgow or Edinburgh will cost at least £150-200 return. The flight from London to Glasgow and Edinburgh is roughly one hour.

There are flight to Inverness from London and from many regional UK airports, as well as flights from Glasgow to Islay, Tiree, Barra, Benbecula, Stornoway, Kirkwall (Orkney) and Sumburgh (Shetland), from Edinburgh to Wick, Stornoway, Kirkwall and Sumburgh and from Inverness to Benbecula, Stornoway, Kirkwall and Sumburgh with Flybe franchise partner, Loganair (www.flybe.com or www.loganair.co.uk). For full details of all flights to Highlands and Islands airports from the rest of the UK, visit the **Highlands and Islands Airports Ltd** website, www.hial.co.uk.

From the rest of Europe There are direct flights to **Glasgow International** from many European capitals, including Copenhagen, Amsterdam, Paris (Beauvais), Dublin, Frankfurt, Stockholm, Brussels, Milan, Oslo and Barcelona. There are flights to **Edinburgh** from Paris (CDG), Zurich, Amsterdam, Brussels, Copenhagen and Frankfurt; direct flights to **Aberdeen** from Amsterdam, Copenhagen and Stavanger; and to **Inverness** from Amsterdam and Zurich.

From North America Because of the much larger number of flights to London, it is generally cheaper to fly there first and get an onward flight, see above for the best deals. For low season Apex fares, expect to pay around US$500-700 from New York and other East Coast cities, and around US$700-900 from the West Coast. Prices rise to around US$700-1000 from New York, and up to US$1000 from the West Coast in the summer months. Low season Apex fares from

Toronto and Montreal cost around CAN$700-900, and from Vancouver around CAN$800-900, rising during the summer. East Coast USA to Glasgow takes around six to seven hours direct. To London it takes seven hours. From the West Coast it takes an additional four hours.

To Glasgow International **Continental Airlines** and **KLM** fly from New York, **Aer Lingus** and **KLM** fly from Chicago and **Air Canada** from Toronto.

Airport information **Glasgow International** ① *T0844-481 5555*, is 8 miles west of the city, at junction 28 on the M8. It handles domestic and international flights. Terminal facilities include car hire, bank ATMs, currency exchange, left luggage, tourist information (T0141-848 4440), and shops, restaurants and bars. For all public transport information T0871-200 2233. **Edinburgh airport** ① *T0844-4812 8989 for general enquiries*, has all facilities, including a tourist information desk, currency exchange, ATMs, restaurants and bars (first floor), shops (ground floor and first floor) and car hire desks in the terminal in the main UK arrivals area. For details of facilities and amenties at all Highlands and Islands airports, visit www.hial.co.uk.

Rail
There are fast and frequent rail services from London and other main towns and cities in England to Glasgow, Edinburgh, Aberdeen and Inverness. Journey time from London is about 4½ hours to Edinburgh, five hours to Glasgow, seven hours to Aberdeen and eight hours to Inverness. Two companies operate direct services from London to Scotland: **National Express** trains leave from King's Cross and run up the east coast to Edinburgh, Aberdeen and Inverness, and **Virgin** trains leave from Euston and run up the west coast to Glasgow. **ScotRail** operate the *Caledonian Sleeper* service if you wish to travel overnight from London Euston to Aberdeen, Edinburgh, Glasgow, Inverness and Fort William. This runs nightly from Sunday to Friday. Fare start from £59 per person. For more information, see www.scotrail.co.uk or the excellent www.seat61.com.

Eurostar ① *T08705-186186 (+44-123-361 7575), www.eurostar.com*, operates high-speed trains through the Channel Tunnel to London St Pancras International from Paris (2½ hours), Brussels (two hours) and Lille (1½ hours). You then have to change trains, and stations, for the onward journey north to Scotland. If you're driving from continental Europe you could take *Le Shuttle*, which runs 24 hours a day, 365 days a year, and takes you and your car from Calais to Folkestone in 35 to 45 minutes. Standard return fares on *Le Shuttle* range from £98 per carload. Depending on how far in advance you book, or when you travel, cheaper fares are available, call T08705-353535 for bookings.

Enquiries and booking **National Rail Enquiries** ① *T08457-484950, www.nationalrail.co.uk*, are quick and courteous with information on rail services and fares but not always accurate, so double check. They can't book tickets but will provide you with the relevant telephone number. The website, www.qjump.co.uk, is a bit hit-and-miss but generally fast and efficient, and shows you all the various options on any selected journey, while www.thetrainline.co.uk, also has its idiosyncrasies but shows prices clearly. For advance card bookings, contact **National Express**, T08457-484950, www.nationalexpresseastcoast.com; **ScotRail**, T08457-550033, www.scotrail.co.uk; and **Virgin**, T08457-222333, www.virgintrains.co.uk.

Fares To describe the system of rail ticket pricing as complicated is a huge understatement and impossible to explain here. There are many and various discounted fares, but restrictions are often prohibitive, which explains the long queues and delays at ticket counters in railway stations. The cheapest ticket is an Advance ticket or Value Advance (Virgin), which must be booked in advance (obviously), though this is not available on all journeys. A GNER London–Edinburgh Advance Single costs between £14-100. Advance Singles with ScotRail on this route start from £39.50 for direct trains. All discount tickets should be booked as quickly as possible as they are often sold out weeks, or even months, in advance. A Caledonian Sleeper 'Bargain Berth' single ticket from London to Edinburgh or Glasgow costs from £19; to book visit www.travelpass.buytickets.scotrail.co.uk.

Railcards There are a variety of railcards which give discounts on fares for certain groups. Cards are valid for one year and most are available from main stations. You need two passport photos and proof of age or status.

Young Person's Railcard For those aged 16-25 or full-time students aged 26+ in the UK. Costs £26 for one year and gives 33% discount on most train tickets and some other services (www.16-25railcard.co.uk).

Senior Citizen's Railcard For those aged over 60. Same price and discounts as above (www.senior-railcard.co.uk).

Disabled Person's Railcard Costs £18 and gives 33% discount to a disabled person and one other. Pick up an application form from stations and send it to Disabled Person's Railcard Office, PO Box 163, Newcastle-upon-Tyne, NE12 8WX. It may take up to 21 days to process, so apply in advance (www.disabledpersons-railcard.co.uk).

Family Railcard Costs £26 and gives 33% discount on most tickets for up to four adults travelling together, and 60% discount for up to four children.

Road

Bus/coach Road links to Scotland are excellent, and a number of companies offer express coach services day and night. This is the cheapest form of travel to Scotland. The main operator between England and Scotland is **National Express** ① T08717-818178, www.national express.com. There are direct buses from most British cities to Edinburgh, Glasgow, Aberdeen and Inverness. Tickets can be bought at bus stations or from a huge number of agents throughout the country. Fares from London to Glasgow and Edinburgh with **National Express** start at around £25 return for a Funfare return (online discount fare). Fares to Aberdeen and Inverness are a little higher. The London to Glasgow/Edinburgh journey takes around eight hours, while it takes around 11 to 12 hours for the trip to Aberdeen and Inverness. From Manchester to Glasgow takes around 6½ hours.

Car There are two main routes to Scotland from the south. In the east the A1 runs to Edinburgh and in the west the M6 and A74(M) runs to Glasgow. The journey north from London to either city takes around eight to 10 hours. The A74(M) route to Glasgow is dual carriageway all the way. A slower and more scenic route is to head off the A1 and take the A68 through the Borders to Edinburgh. There's an Autoshuttle Express service to transport your car overnight between England and Scotland and vice versa while you travel by rail or air. For further information and reservations, T08705-502309. See also page 10.

Sea P&O Irish Sea ① T0871-664 2020, www.poferries.com, has several crossings daily from Larne to Cairnryan (one hour), and from Larne to Troon (two hours). Fares are from £79 each way for for car and driver. **Stena Line** ① T0870-570 7070, www.stenaline.co.uk, runs numerous ferries (three hours) and high-speed catamarans (1½ hours) from Belfast to Stranraer, fares from £79 single for car and driver.

Getting around

It is easy to visit the main towns and tourist sights by bus or train, but getting off the beaten track without your own transport requires careful planning and an intimate knowledge of rural bus timetables. Public transport can also be expensive, though there's a whole raft of discount passes and tickets which can save you a lot of money. Hiring a car can work out as a more economical, and certainly more flexible, option, especially for more than two people travelling together. It will also enable you to get off the beaten track and see more of the country. Even if you're driving, however, getting around the remote Highlands and Islands can be a time-consuming business as much of the region is accessed only by a sparse network of tortuous, twisting single-track roads. Be sure to refuel regularly, allow plenty of time for getting around and book ferries in advance during the busy summer season.

Air

As well as the main airports of Glasgow, Edinburgh, Aberdeen and Inverness, there are also numerous small airports, many of them on islands (one of them, on Barra, uses the beach as an airstrip). Internal flights are relatively expensive, however, and not really necessary in such a small country, unless you are short of time. For example a return flight from Edinburgh or Glasgow to Shetland can cost over £200. There are discounted tickets available, which must be booked at least 14 days in advance, and special offers on some services. There is no departure tax on flights from Highlands and Islands airports.

The majority of flights are operated by **Flybe/Loganair** ① *T0871-700 2000, www.fly be.com, www.loganair.co.uk*. For inter-island flights in Orkney, you should book direct through **Loganair**, T01856-873457. For information on flight schedules, call the airports listed on page 7, or **British Airways**. The British Airports Authority (BAA) publishes a free *Scheduled Flight Guide*.

Rail

The rail network in Scotland is limited and train travel is comparatively expensive, but trains are a fast and effective way to get around and also provide some beautifully scenic journeys. The West Highland line to Fort William and Mallaig and the journey from Inverness to Kyle of Lochalsh are amongst the most beautiful rail journeys in the world and well worth doing. Services between Glasgow, Edinburgh, Stirling, Perth, Dundee and Aberdeen are fast and frequent, and there are frequent trains to and from Inverness.

ScotRail operates most train services within Scotland. You can buy train tickets at the stations, from major travel agents, or over the phone with a credit or debit card. For information and advance credit or debit card bookings visit www.scotrail.co.uk. Details of services are given throughout the guide. For busy long-distance routes it's best to reserve a seat. Seat reservations to Edinburgh, Glasgow, Aberdeen or Inverness are included in the price of the ticket when you book in advance. If the ticket office is closed, there's usually a machine on the platform. If this isn't working, you can buy a ticket on the train. Cyclists should note that though train companies have a more relaxed attitude to taking bikes on trains, reservations at a small fee for bikes are still required on some services. Cycles are carried free of charge on ScotRail services, although reservations are required on longer distance routes.

Eurorail passes are not recognized in Britain, but **ScotRail** offers a couple of worthwhile travel passes. The most flexible is the **Freedom of Scotland Travelpass**, which gives unlimited rail travel within Scotland. It is also valid on all **CalMac** ferries on the west coast, many **Citylink** bus services in the Highlands, some regional buses and offers discounts on some city centre bus tours. It also gives 20% discount on **Northlink Ferries** between Scrabster–Stromness, Aberdeen–Lerwick and Aberdeen–Kirkwall–Lerwick. It costs £114 for four days' travel out of eight consecutive days, £153 for eight out of 15. The **Highland Rover** and Central Scotland Rover Tickets are more limited. The Highland Rover allows unlimited rail travel in the Highlands region, plus the West Highland line from Glasgow, and travel between Aberdeen and Aviemore. It also allows free travel on **Citylink** buses between Oban, Fort William and Inverness. Ferry travel between Oban–Mull and Mallaig–Skye is also included on this ticket. It costs £74 for any four out of eight consecutive days. The Central Scotland Rover allows unlimited travel in the central belt of Scotland from the East Coast, Edinburgh, Stirling and Fife to Glasgow, and also covers unlimited travel on the Glasgow Underground network. It costs £33 for any three out of seven consecutive days.

Road

Bus and coach Travelling around Scotland by bus takes longer than the train but is much cheaper. There are numerous local bus companies, but the main operator is **Scottish Citylink** ① T08705-505050, www.citylink.co.uk. Bus services between towns and cities are good, but far less frequent in more remote rural areas. To identify bus times and the myriad of operators in the Highlands it's worthwhile visiting www.rapsons.co.uk, and downloading the relevant timetable. Note that long-distance express buses are called coaches. There are a number of discount and flexible tickets available and details of these are given on the **Citylink** website, which is fast and easy to use.

Available to overseas passport holders, the **Brit Xplorer Pass** offers unlimited travel on all **National Express** buses. Passes cost from £79 for seven days, £139 for 14 days and £219 for its month-long Rolling Stone pass. They can be bought from major airports and bus terminals. **Scottish Citylink** runs a daily bus service between Scotland's six cities and strategic ports including Oban, Uig (Skye) and Ullapool. It offers a diverse range of discount and saver cards including an Explorer Pass that offers unlimited travel on its routes for a specified number of days. Passes start from £35 for three days.

Many parts of the Highlands and Islands can only be reached by Royal Mail **postbuses**. Admittedly, in recent years many routes have disappeared to be replaced by Dial-a-Bus services, such as in Gairloch. These operate on demand and don't follow a fixed timetable, see www.highland.gov.uk or www.royalmail.com/postbus. However, in places you can still find the friendly, red postbus. These are minibuses that follow postal delivery routes and carry up to 14 fare-paying passengers. They set off early in the morning from the main post office and follow a circuitous route as they deliver and collect mail in the most far-flung places. They are often very slow on the outward morning routes but quicker on the return routes in the afternoons. It can be a slow method of getting around, but you get to see some of the country's most beautiful scenery, and it is useful for walkers and those trying to reach remote hostels or B&Bs. There's a restricted service on Saturdays and none on Sundays.

Car and campervan Travelling with your own private transport is the ideal way to explore the country, particularly the Highlands. This allows you to cover a lot of ground in a short space of time and to reach remote places. The main disadvantages are rising fuel costs (around £1.50 per litre for diesel), traffic congestion and parking, but the latter two are only a problem in the main cities and on the motorways in the Central Belt. Roads in the Highlands and Islands are a lot less busy than those in England, and driving is relatively stress-free, especially on the B-roads and minor roads. In more remote parts of the country, on the islands in particular, many roads are single track, with passing places indicated by a diamond-shaped signpost. These should also be used to allow traffic behind you to overtake. Remember that you may want to take your time to enjoy the stupendous views all around you, but the driver behind may be a local doctor in a hurry. Don't park in passing places. A major driving hazard on single track roads are the huge number of sheep wandering around, blissfully unaware of your presence. When confronted by a flock of sheep, slow down and gently edge your way past. Be particularly careful at night, as many of them sleep by the side of the road (counting cars perhaps). Also keep a sharp lookout for deer, particularly at night.

To drive in Scotland you must have a current **driving licence**. Foreign nationals also need an international **driving permit**, available from state and national motoring organizations for a small fee. Those importing their own vehicle should also have their vehicle registration or ownership document. Make sure you're adequately **insured**. In all of the UK you drive on the left. **Speed limits** are 30 miles per hour (mph) in built-up areas, 70 mph on motorways and dual carriageways, and 60 mph on most other roads.

It's advisable to join one of the main UK motoring organizations during your visit for their 24-hour breakdown assistance. The two main ones in Britain are the **Automobile Association** (**AA**) ① *T0800-085 2721, www.theaa.com,* and the **Royal Automobile Club** (**RAC**) ① *T08705-722722, www.rac.co.uk.* One year's membership of the AA starts at £30 and £28 for the RAC. They also provide many other services, including a reciprocal agreement for free assistance with many overseas motoring organizations. Check to see if your organization is included. Both companies can also extend their cover to include Europe. Their emergency numbers are: **AA**, T0800-887766; **RAC**, T0800-828282. You can call these numbers even if you're not a member, but you'll have to a pay a large fee. In remote areas you may have to wait a long time for assistance. Also note that in the Highlands and Islands you may be stranded for ages waiting for spare parts to arrive.

Car hire need not be expensive in Scotland if you shop around for the best deals. **AVIS** (see below) offers weekend rates from around £45 and £126 for the week, though whichever operator you choose be wary of high charges for additional mileage. Even without deals you should be able to hire a small car for a week from £150. Local hire companies often offer better deals than the larger multi-nationals, though **easyCar** can offer the best rates, at around £10 per day, if you book in advance and don't push up the charges with high mileage. They are based at Aberdeen, Glasgow, Edinburgh and Inverness airport. Many companies such as **Europcar** offer the flexibility of picking up in Glasgow and leaving in Edinburgh, and vice versa. Most companies prefer payment with a credit card, otherwise you'll have to leave a large deposit (£100 or more). You'll need a full driver's licence (one or two years) and be aged over 21 (23 in some cases).

Alternatively, why not hire your own transport and accommodation at the same time by renting a campervan. Campervans can be rented from a number of companies and it's best to arrange this before arriving as everything gets booked up in the high season (June-August). Inverness based **Highland Camper Vans** is a good bet with its new two-berth 'Adventure Van' starting at around £385 per week and £75 per day, or £525 per week for its four-person touring van.

Hitching As in the rest of the UK, hitching is never entirely safe, and is certainly not advised for anyone travelling alone, particularly women travellers. Those prepared to take the risk should not find it too difficult to get a lift in the Highlands and Islands, where people are far more willing to stop for you. Bear in mind, though, that you will probably have to wait a while even to see a vehicle in some parts.

Sleeping

Staying in the Highlands and Islands of Scotland can mean anything from being pampered to within an inch of your life in a baronial mansion to roughing it in a tiny island bothy with no electricity. If you have the money, then the sky is very much the limit in terms of sheer splendour and excess. We have listed many of the top class establishments in this book, with a bias towards those that offer that little bit extra in terms of character. Those spending less may have to forego the four-posters and Egyptian cotton sheets but there are still many good-value small hotels and guesthouses with that essential wow factor – especially when it comes to the views. At the bottom end of the scale, there are also some excellent hostels in some pretty special locations.

We have tried to give as broad a selection as possible to cater for all tastes and budgets but if you can't find what you're after, or if someone else has beaten you to the draw, then the tourist information centres (TICs) will help find accommodation for you. They can recommend a place within your particular budget and give you the number to phone up and book yourself, or will book a room for you. Some offices charge a small fee (usually £1) for booking a room, while others ask you to pay a deposit of 10% which is deducted from your first night's bill. Details of town and city TICs are given throughout the guide. There are also several websites that you can browse and book accommodation. Try www. visitscotland.com, www.scottishaccommodationindex.com, www.aboutscotland.com, www.scotland200.com, and www.assc.co.uk.

Accommodation in Scotland will be your greatest expense, particularly if you are travelling on your own. Single rooms are in short supply and many places are reluctant to let a double room to one person, even when they're not busy. Single rooms are usually more than the cost per person for a double room and in some cases cost the same as two people sharing a double room.

Hotels, guesthouses and B&Bs

Area tourist boards publish accommodation lists that include campsites, hostels, self-catering accommodation and VisitScotland-approved hotels, guesthouses and bed and breakfasts (B&Bs). Places participating in the VisitScotland system will have a plaque displayed outside which shows their grading, determined by a number of stars ranging from one to five. These reflect the level of facilities, as well as the quality of hospitality and service. However, do not assume that a B&B, guesthouse or hotel is no good because it is not listed by the tourist board. They simply don't want to pay to be included in the system, and some of them may offer better value. If you'd like to stay in a Scottish castle as a paying guest of the owner, contact **Scotts Castle Holidays** ⓘ *T01208-821341, www.scottscastles.com*.

Hotels At the top end of the scale there are some fabulously luxurious hotels, often in spectacular locations. Many of them are converted baronial mansions or castles, and offer a chance to enjoy a taste of aristocratic grandeur and style. At the lower end of the scale, there is often little to choose between cheaper hotels and guesthouses or B&Bs. The latter often offer higher standards of comfort and a more personal service, but many smaller hotels are really just guesthouses, and are often family-run and every bit as friendly. Note that some hotels, especially in town centres or in fishing ports, may also be rather noisy, as the bar can often be the social hub. Rooms in most mid-range to expensive hotels almost always have bathrooms en suite. Many upmarket hotels offer excellent room-only deals in the low season. An efficient last-minute hotel booking service is www.laterooms.com,

Sleeping and eating price codes

Sleeping

££££ £160 and over   **£££** £90-160   **££** £50-90
£ under £50

Prices include taxes and service charge, but not meals. They are based on a double room, except in the $ range, where prices are almost always per person.

Eating price codes

♈♈♈ over £20 a head   **♈♈** £10-20   **♈** under £10 a head

Prices refer to the cost of a two-course meal for one person, excluding drinks or service charge.

which specializes in weekend breaks. Also note that many hotels offer cheaper rates for online booking through agencies such as www.lastminute.com.

Guesthouses Guesthouses are often large, converted family homes with up to five or six rooms. They tend to be slightly more expensive than B&Bs, charging between £30 and £50 per person per night, and though they are often less personal, usually provide better facilities, such as en suite bathroom, colour TV in each room and private parking. In many instances they are more like small budget hotels. Many guesthouses offer evening meals, though this may have to be requested in advance.

Bed and breakfasts (B&Bs) B&Bs provide the cheapest private accommodation. At the bottom end of the scale you can get a bedroom in a private house, a shared bathroom and a huge cooked breakfast for around £20-25 per person per night. Small B&Bs may only have one or two rooms to let, so it's important to book in advance during the summer season and on the islands where accommodation options are more limited. More upmarket B&Bs have en suite bathrooms and TVs in each room and usually charge from £25-35 per person per night. In general, B&Bs are more hospitable, informal, friendlier and offer better value than hotels. Many B&B owners are also a great source of local knowledge and can even provide OS maps for local walks. B&Bs in the Outer Hebrides and other remote locations also offer dinner, bed and breakfast, which is useful as eating options are limited, especially on a Sunday.

Some places, especially in ferry ports, charge room-only rates, which are slightly cheaper and allow you to get up in time to catch an early morning ferry. However, this means that you miss out on a huge cooked breakfast. If you're travelling on a tight budget, you can eat as much as you can at breakfast time and save on lunch as you won't need to eat again until evening. This is particularly useful if you're heading into the hills, as you won't have to carry so much food. Many B&B owners will even make up a packed lunch for you at a small extra cost.

Hostels

For those travelling on a tight budget, there is a large network of hostels offering cheap accommodation. These are also popular centres for backpackers and provide a great opportunity for meeting fellow travellers. Hostels have kitchen facilities for self-catering, and some include a continental breakfast in the price or provide cheap breakfasts and evening meals. Advance booking is recommended at all times, particularly from May to September and on public holidays, and a credit card is often useful.

Scottish Youth Hostel Association (SYHA) The **Scottish Youth Hostel Association (SYHA)** ① *7 Glebe Cres, Stirling, T01786-891400, www.syha.org.uk*, is separate from the YHA in England and Wales. It has a network of over 60 hostels, which are often better and cheaper than those in other countries. They offer bunk-bed accommodation in single-sex dormitories or smaller rooms, kitchen and laundry facilities. The average cost is £10-20 per person per night. Though some rural hostels are still strict on discipline and impose a 2300 curfew, those in larger towns and cities tend to be more relaxed and doors are closed as late as 0200. Some larger hostels provide breakfasts for around £2.50 and three-course evening meals for £4-5. For all EU residents, adult membership costs £10, and can be obtained at the SYHA National Office, or at the first SYHA hostel you stay at. SYHA membership gives automatic membership of Hostelling International (HI). The SYHA produces a handbook (free with membership) giving details of all their youth hostels, including transport links. This can be useful as some hostels are difficult to get to without your own transport. You should always phone ahead, as many hostels are closed during the day and phone numbers are listed in this guide. Many hostels are closed during the winter, details are given in the SYHA Handbook. Youth hostel members are entitled to various discounts, including 20% off Edinburgh bus tours, 20% off Scottish Citylink tickets and 33% off the Orkney Bus (Inverness–Kirkwall).

Independent hostels Details of most independent hostels (or 'bunkhouses') can be found in the annual Independent Hostel Guide, www.independenthostelguide.com. The Independent Backpackers Hostels of Scotland is an association of nearly 100 independent hostels/bunkhouses throughout Scotland. This association has a programme of inspection and lists members in their free '*Blue Guide*'. Independent hostels tend to be more laid-back, with fewer rules and no curfew, and no membership is required. They all have dormitories, hot showers and self-catering kitchens. Some include continental breakfast, or provide cheap breakfasts. All these hostels are listed on their excellent website, www.hostel-scotland.co.uk.

Campsites and self-catering
Campsites There are hundreds of campsites around Scotland. They are mostly geared to caravans, and vary greatly in quality and level of facilities. The most expensive sites, which charge up to £15 to pitch a tent, are usually well-equipped. Sites are usually only open from April to October. If you plan to do a lot of camping, you should check out www.scottish camping.com, which is the most comprehensive service with over 500 sites, many with pictures and reviews from punters. North Americans planning on camping should invest in an international camping carnet, which is available from home motoring organizations, or from **Family Campers and RVers (FCRV)** ① *4804 Transit Rd, Building 2, Depew, NY 14043, T1-800-245 9755, www.fcrv.org*. It gives you discounts at member sites.

Self-catering One of the most cost-effective ways to holiday in the Highlands and Islands is to hire a cottage with a group of friends. There are lots of different types of accommodation to choose from, to suit all budgets, ranging from luxury lodges, castles and lighthouses to basic bothies with no electricity. The minimum stay is usually one week in the summer peak season, though many offer shorter stays of two, three or four nights, especially outside the peak season. Expect to pay at least £200-400 per week for a two-bedroom cottage in the winter, rising to £400-1000 in the high season, or more if it's a particularly nice place. A good source of self-catering accommodation is the VisitScotland's guide, which lists over 1200 properties and is available to buy from any tourist office, but there are also dozens of excellent websites to browse. Amongst the best websites are the following: www.cottages-and- castles.co.uk; www.

Pitch a tent on the wild side

The Land Reform (Scotland) Act 2003, which together with the Scottish Access Code came into effect in February 2005, ensures Scotland offers walkers, canoeists, cyclists and campers some of the most liberal land access laws in Europe. Technically it means you have the 'right to roam' almost anywhere, although the emphasis is on 'responsible access' (see www.outdooraccess-scotland.com).

scottish-country-cottages.co.uk; www.cottages4you.co.uk; www.rural retreats.co.uk, www.assc.co.uk. If you want to tickle a trout or feed a pet lamb, www.farm stay.co.uk, offer over a thousand good value rural places to stay around the UK, all clearly listed on a clickable map.

The **National Trust for Scotland** ① *28 Charlotte Sq, Edinburgh, T0844-493 2100, www.nts.org.uk*, owns many historic properties which are available for self-catering holidays, sleeping between two and 15 people. Prices start at around £300 per week in high season rising to £1000 for the top of the range lodges.

Eating and drinking

While Scotland's national drink is loved the world over, Scottish cooking hasn't exactly had good press over the years. This is perhaps not too surprising, as the national dish, haggis, consists of a stomach stuffed with diced innards and served with mashed tatties (potatoes) and *neeps* (turnips). Not a great start. And things got even worse when the Scots discovered the notorious deep-fried Mars bar.

However, Scottish cuisine has undergone a dramatic transformation in the last decade and Scotland now boasts some of the most talented chefs, creating some of the best food in Britain. The heart of Scottish cooking is local produce, which includes the finest fish, shellfish, game, lamb, beef and vegetables, and a vast selection of traditionally made cheeses. What makes Scottish cooking so special is ready access to these foods. What could be better than enjoying an aperitif whilst watching your dinner being delivered by a local fisherman, knowing that an hour later you'll be enjoying the most delicious seafood?

Modern Scottish cuisine is now a feature of many of the top restaurants in the country. This generally means the use of local ingredients with foreign-influenced culinary styles, in particular French. International cuisine is also now a major feature on menus all over the country, influenced by the rise of Indian and Chinese restaurants in recent decades. In fact, so prevalent are exotic Asian and Oriental flavours that curry has now replaced fish and chips (fish supper) as the nation's favourite food.

Food

Fish, meat and game form the base of many of the country's finest dishes. Scottish beef, particularly Aberdeen Angus, is the most famous in the world. This will, or should, usually be hung for at least four weeks and sliced thick. Game is also a regular feature of Scottish menus, though it can be expensive, especially venison (deer), but delicious and low in cholesterol. Pheasant and hare are also tasty, but grouse is, quite frankly, overrated.

Fish and seafood are fresh and plentiful, and if you're travelling around the northwest coast you must not miss the chance to savour local mussels, prawns, oysters, scallops, langoustines, lobster or crab. Salmon is, of course, the most famous of Scottish fish, but you're more likely to be served the fish-farmed variety than 'wild' salmon, which has a more delicate flavour. Trout is also farmed extensively, but the standard of both remains high. Kippers are also a favourite delicacy, the best of which come from Loch Fyne or the Achiltibuie smokery, see page 271. Proper fish and chips in Scotland are made with haddock; cod is for Sassenachs (the English) and cats.

Haggis has made something of a comeback, and small portions are often served as starters in fashionable restaurants. Haggis is traditionally eaten on Burns Night (25 January) in celebration of the great poet's birthday, when it is piped to the table and then slashed open with a sword at the end of a recital of Robert Burns' *Address to the Haggis*. Other national favourites feature names to relish: **cock-a-leekie** is a soup made from chicken, leeks and prunes; **cullen skink** is a delicious concoction of smoked haddock and potatoes; while at the other end of the scale of appeal is **hugga-muggie**, a Shetland dish using fish's stomach. There's also the delightfully named **crappit heids** (haddock heads stuffed with lobster) and **partan bree** (a soup made form giant crab's claws, cooked with rice). Rather more mundane is the ubiquitous **Scotch broth**, made with mutton stock, vegetables, barley, lentils and split peas, and **stovies**, which is a hearty mash of potato, onion and minced beef.

Waist-expanding puddings or desserts are a very important part of Scottish cooking and often smothered in butterscotch sauce or syrup. There is a huge variety, including **cranachan**, a mouth-watering mix of toasted oatmeal steeped in whisky, cream and fresh raspberries, and **Atholl Brose**, a similar confection of oatmeal, whisky and cream.

Eaten before pudding, in the French style, or afterwards, are Scotland's many home-produced cheeses, which have made a successful comeback in the face of mass-produced varieties. Many of the finest cheeses are produced on the islands, especially Arran, Mull, Islay and Orkney. **Caboc** is a creamy soft cheese rolled in oatmeal and is made in the Highlands.

Anyone staying at a hotel, guesthouse or B&B will experience the hearty **Scottish breakfast**, which includes bacon, egg, sausage, 'tattie scone' and black pudding (a type of sausage made with blood), all washed down with copious quantities of tea. Coffee is readily available everywhere, with most places now offering a selection of cappuccinos and café lattes. You may also be served kippers (smoked herring) or porridge, an erstwhile Scottish staple. Made with oatmeal and with the consistency of Italian polenta, it is traditionally eaten with salt, though heretics are offered sugar instead. Oatcakes (oatmeal biscuits) may also be on offer, as well as potato scones, baps (bread rolls) or bannocks (a sort of large oatcake). After such a huge cooked breakfast you probably won't feel like eating again until dinner.

Drink

Beer Beer is the alcoholic drink of choice in Scotland. The most popular type of beer is lager, which is generally brewed in the UK, even when it bears the name of an overseas brand, and is almost always weaker in both strength and character than the lagers in mainland Europe. However, examples of the older and usually darker type of beers, known as ales, are still widely available, and connoisseurs should try some of these as they are far more rewarding. Indeed, the best of them rival Scotland's whiskies as gourmet treats.

Traditionally, Scottish ales were graded by the shilling, an old unit of currency written as /-, according to strength. This system is still widely used by the older established breweries, though many of the newer independents and 'micros' have departed from it. 70/- beers at around 3.5% ABV (alcohol by volume), known as 'heavy', and 80/- beers (4.5% sometimes known as 'export'), are the most popular, while 60/-, 'light' (3-3.5%) is harder to find. Very strong 90/- beers (6.5% + ABV), known as 'wee heavies', are also brewed, mainly for bottling.

The market is dominated by the giant international brewers: Scottish Courage with its McEwans and Youngers brands; Interbrew with Calders and Carslberg; and Tetley with Tennents lagers. Tennents was the first British brewery to produce a continental-style lager commercially back in the 19th century, and, despite a competitive marketplace, remains a favourite for many Scots.

Much better are the ales from smaller independent breweries. Edinburgh's Caledonian is a world-class brewer producing many excellent beers, including a popular 80/- and a renowned golden hoppy ale, Deuchars IPA. Belhaven, an old, established family brewery in Dunbar, has some superb traditional beers including a malty 80/-, once marketed as the Burgundy of Scotland. Broughton, a microbrewery in the Borders, produces the fruity Greenmantle and an oatmeal stout. Another micro, Harvieston of Clackmannanshire (once an important brewing country) offers a wide and adventurous range of specialities, including Ptarmigan 80/- and a naturally brewed cask lager, Schiehallion. The Heather Ale Company, near Glasgow, has the spicy, unusual Fraoch (pronounced 'Frooch'), which is flavoured with real heather and hops.

Draught beer in pubs and bars is served in pints, or half pints, and you'll pay between £2.50 and £3.50 for a pint (unless you discover a 'Happy Hour' offering good deals on drinks, usually for much more than one hour! Happy hours usually apply in late afternoon or early evening). In many pubs the basic ales are chilled under gas pressure like lagers, but the best ales, such as those from the independents, are 'real ales', still fermenting in the cask and served cool but not chilled (around 12°C) under natural pressure from a handpump, electric pump or air pressure fount. All Scottish beers are traditionally served with a full, creamy head.

Whisky No visit to the Scottish Highlands would be complete without availing oneself of a 'wee dram'. There is no greater pleasure on an inclement evening than enjoying a malt whisky in front of a roaring log fire whilst watching the rain outside pelt down relentlessly. The roots of Scotland's national drink (*uisge beatha*, or 'water of life' in Gaelic) go back to the late 15th century, but it wasn't until the invention of a patent still in the early 19th century that distilling began to develop from small family-run operations to the large manufacturing business it has become today. Now more than 700 million bottles a year are exported, mainly to the United States, France, Japan and Spain.

There are two types of whisky: single malt, made only from malted barley; and grain, which is made from malted barley together with unmalted barley, maize or other cereals, and is faster and cheaper to produce. Most of the popular brands are blends of both types of whisky – usually 60-70% grain to 30-40% malt. These blended whiskies account for over 90% of all sales worldwide, and most of the production of single malts is used to add flavour to a blended whisky. Amongst the best-known brands of blended whisky are Johnnie Walker, Bells, Teachers and Famous Grouse. There's not much between them in terms of flavour and they are usually drunk with a mixer, such as water or soda.

Single malts are a different matter altogether. Each is distinctive and should be drunk neat to appreciate fully its subtle flavours, though some believe that the addition of water helps free the flavours. Single malts vary enormously. Their distinctive flavours and aromas are derived from the peat used for drying, the water used for mashing, the type of oak cask used and the location of the distillery. Single malts fall into four groups: Highland, Lowland, Campbeltown and Islay. There are over 40 distilleries to choose from, most offering guided tours. The majority are located around Speyside, in the northeast. The region's many distilleries include that perennial favourite, Glenfiddich, which is sold in 185 countries. Recommended alternatives are the produce of the beautiful and peaceful Isle of Islay, whose malts are lovingly described in terms of their peaty quality and the produce of the island known as 'Scotland in Miniature', Arran, whose 10-year-old malt, distilled in Lochranza, has won recent international acclaim. Scots tend to favour the 10-year-old Glenmorangie, while the most popular in the USA is The Macallan.

Turn water into whisky

Malt whisky is made by first soaking dry barley in tanks of local water for two to three days. Then the barley is spread out on a concrete floor or placed in cylindrical drums and allowed to germinate for between eight and 12 days, after which it is dried in a kiln, heated by a peat fire. Next, the dried malt is ground and mixed with hot water in a huge circular vat called a 'mash tun'. A sugary liquid called 'wort' is then drawn from the porridge-like result and piped into huge containers where living yeast is stirred into the mix in order to convert the sugar in the wort into alcohol. After about 48 hours the 'wash' is transferred to copper pot stills and heated till the alcohol vaporizes and is then condensed by a cooling plant into distilled alcohol which is passed through a second still. Once distilled, the liquid is poured into oak casks and left to age for a minimum of three years, though a good malt will stay casked for at least eight years.

Eating out

There are places to suit every taste and budget. In the large towns and cities you'll find a vast selection of eating places, including Indian, Chinese, Italian and French restaurants, as well as Thai, Japanese, Mexican, Spanish and, of course Scottish, but beyond the main cities, choice is much more limited. More and more restaurants are moving away from national culinary boundaries and offering a wide range of international dishes and flavours, so you'll often find Latin American, Oriental and Pacific Rim dishes all on the same menu. This is particularly the case in the many continental-style bistros, brasseries and café-bars, which now offer a more informal alternative to traditional restaurants. Vegetarians are increasingly well catered for, especially in the large cities, where exclusively vegetarian/vegan restaurants and cafés are often the cheapest places to eat. Outside the cities, vegetarian restaurants are thin on the ground, though better-quality eating places will normally offer a reasonable vegetarian selection.

For a cheap meal, your best bet is a pub, hotel bar or café, where you can have a one-course meal for around £5-7 or less, though don't expect gourmet food. The best value is often at lunchtime, when many restaurants offer three-course set lunches or business lunches for less than £10. You'll need a pretty huge appetite to feel like eating a three-course lunch after your gigantic cooked breakfast, however. Also good value are the pre-theatre dinners offered by many restaurants in the larger towns and cities (you don't need to have a theatre ticket to take advantage). These are usually available from around 1730-1800 until 1900-1930, so you could get away with just a sandwich for lunch. At the other end of the price scale are many excellent restaurants where you can enjoy the finest of Scottish cuisine, often with a continental influence, and these are often found in hotels. You can expect to pay from around £30 a head up to £40 or £50 (excluding drinks) in the very top establishments.

The biggest problem with eating out in Scotland, as in the rest of the UK, is the ludicrously limited serving hours in some pubs and hotels, particularly in remoter locations. These places only serve food during restricted hours, seemingly ignorant of the eating habits of foreign visitors, or those who would prefer a bit more flexibility during their holiday. In small places especially, it can be difficult finding food outside these enforced times. Places that serve food all day till 2100 or later are restaurants, fast-food outlets and the many chic bistros and café-bars, which can be found not only in the main cities but increasingly in smaller towns. The latter often offer very good value and above-average quality fare.

Essentials A-Z

Accident and emergency
For police, fire brigade, ambulance and, in certain areas, mountain rescue or coastguard, T999 or T112.

Disabled travellers
For travellers with disabilities, visiting Scotland independently can be a difficult business. While most theatres, cinemas, libraries and modern tourist attractions are accessible to wheelchairs, tours of many historic buildings and finding accommodation remains problematic. Many large, new hotels do have disabled suites, but far too many B&Bs, guesthouses and smaller hotels remain ill-equipped to accept bookings from people with disabilities. However, through the work of organizations like **Disability Scotland** the Government is being pressed to further improve the Disability Discrimination Act and access to public amenities and transport. As a result, many buses and FirstScotRail's train services now accommodate wheelchair-users whilst city taxis should carry wheelchair ramps.

Wheelchair users, and blind or partially sighted people are automatically given 30-50% discount on train fares, and those with other disabilities are eligible for the Disabled Person's Railcard, which costs £18 per year and gives a third off most tickets. If you will need assistance at a railway station, call FirstScotRail before travelling on T0800-912 2901. There are no discounts on buses.

If you are disabled you should contact the travel officer of your national support organization. They can provide literature or put you in touch with travel agents specializing in tours for the disabled. **VisitScotland** produces a guide, *Accessible Scotland*, for disabled travellers, and many local tourist offices can provide accessibility details for their area. Alternatively call its national booking hotline on T0845-225

5121. A useful website is www.atlholidays. com, which specializes in organizing holidays for disabled travellers, recommends hotels with good facilities and can also arrange rental cars and taxis.

Useful organizations include:
Capability Scotland, ASCS, 11 Ellersly Rd, Edinburgh EH12 6HY, T0131-313 5510, or Textphone 0131-346 2529, www.capability-scotland.org.uk,

The Holiday Care Service, T0845-124 9974, www.holidaycare.org.uk, www.tourismforall.org.uk. Both websites are excellent sources of information about travel and for identifying accessible accommodation in the UK.

The Royal Association for Disability and Rehabilitation (RADAR), Unit 12, City Forum, 250 City Rd, London EC1V 8AF, T020-7250 3222, www.radar.org.uk. A good source of advice and information. It produces an annual *National Key Scheme Guide* for gaining access to over 6000 toilet facilities across the UK (£10.70 including P&P).

Electricity
The current in Britain is 240V AC. Plugs have 3 square pins and adapters are widely available.

Embassies and consulates
The **Foreign Office** website, www.fco. gov.uk, has a directory of all British embassies overseas.

Health
No vaccinations are required for entry into Britain. Citizens of EU countries are entitled to free medical treatment at National Health Service (NHS) hospitals on production of a European Health Insurance Card (EHIC). For details, see the Department of Health website, www.dh.gov.uk/travellers. Also, Australia, New Zealand and several other

non-EU European countries have reciprocal healthcare arrangements with Britain. Citizens of other countries will have to pay for all medical services, except accident and emergency care given at Accident and Emergency (A&E) Units at most (but not all) National Health Service hospitals. Health insurance is therefore strongly advised for citizens of non-EU countries.

Pharmacists can dispense only a limited range of drugs without a doctor's prescription. Most are open during normal shop hours, though some are open late, especially in larger towns. Local newspapers will carry lists of which are open late. Doctors' surgeries are usually open from around 0830-0900 till 1730-1800, though times vary. Outside surgery hours you can go to the casualty department of the local hospital for any complaint requiring urgent attention. For the address of the nearest hospital or doctors' surgery, www.nhs24.com. See also individual town and city directories throughout the book for details local medical services.

You should encounter no major problems or irritations during your visit to Scotland. The only exceptions are the risk of hyperthermia if you're walking in the mountains in difficult conditions, and the dreaded midge, see box, above.

Money → US$1 = £0.61, €1 = £0.88 (May 2011). The British currency is the pound sterling (£), divided into 100 pence (p). Coins come in denominations of 1p, 2p, 5p, 10p, 20p, 50p, £1 and £2. Bank of England banknotes are legal tender in Scotland, in addition to those issued by the Bank of Scotland, Royal Bank of Scotland and Clydesdale Bank. These Scottish banknotes (bills) come in denominations of £5, £10, £20, £50 and £100 and regardless of what you are told by shopkeepers in England the notes are legal tender in the rest of Britain.

Banks
The larger towns and villages have a branch of at least one of the big 4 high street banks – **Bank of Scotland, Royal Bank of Scotland, Clydesdale** and **TSB Scotland**. Bank opening hours are Mon-Fri from 0930 to between 1600 and 1700. Some larger branches may also be open later on Thu and on Sat mornings. In small and remote places, and on some islands, there may be only a mobile bank which runs to a set timetable. This timetable will be available from the local post office.

Banks are usually the best places to change money and cheques. You can withdraw cash from selected banks and ATMs (or cashpoints as they are called in Britain) with your cash and credit card. Though using a debit or credit card is by far the easiest way of keeping in funds, you must check with your bank what the total charges will be; this can be as high as 4-5% in some cases. In more remote parts, and especially on the islands, ATMs are few and far between and it is important to keep a ready supply of cash on you at all times and many guesthouses in the remoter reaches of Scotland will still request payment in cash. Outside the ferry ports on most of the smaller islands, you won't find an ATM. Your bank will give you a list of locations where you can use your card. **Bank of Scotland** and **Royal Bank** take **Lloyds** and **Barclays** cash cards; **Clydesdale** takes **HSBC** and **National Westminster** cards. **Bank of Scotland, Clydesdale** and most building society cashpoints are part of the Link network and accept all affiliated cards. See also Credit cards below. In addition to ATMs, bureaux de change can be used outside banking hours. These can be found in most city centres and also at the main airports and train stations. Note that some charge high commissions for changing cheques. Those at international airports, however, often charge less than banks and will change pound sterling cheques for free. Avoid changing money or cheques in hotels, as the rates are usually very poor.

Credit cards

Most hotels, shops and restaurants accept the major credit cards such as MasterCard and Visa and, less frequently, Amex, though some places may charge for using them. They may be less useful in more remote rural areas and smaller establishments such as B&Bs, which will often only accept cash or cheques.

Visa card holders can use the **Bank of Scotland**, **Clydesdale Bank**, **Royal Bank of Scotland** and **TSB** ATMs; Access/MasterCard holders the Royal Bank and Clydesdale; Amex card holders the Bank of Scotland.

Traveller's cheques

The safest way to carry money is in traveller's cheques. These are available for a small commission from all major banks. **American Express (Amex)**, **Visa** and **Thomas Cook** cheques are widely accepted and are the most commonly issued by banks. You'll normally have to pay commission again when you cash each cheque. This will usually be 1%, or a flat rate. No commission is payable on Amex cheques cashed at Amex offices, www.americanexpress.co/feefree. Make sure you keep a record of the cheque numbers and the cheques you've cashed separate from the cheques themselves, so that you can get a full refund of all uncashed cheques should you lose them. It's best to bring sterling cheques to avoid changing currencies twice. Also note that in Britain traveller's cheques are rarely accepted outside banks or foreign exchange bureaux, so you'll need to cash them in advance and keep a good supply of ready cash.

Money transfers

If you need money urgently, the quickest way to have it sent to you is to have it wired to the nearest bank via **Western Union**, T0800-833 833, www.westernunion.co.uk, or **Money-gram**, T0800-8971 8971. Charges are on a sliding scale; ie it will cost proportionately less to wire out more money. Money can also be wired by **Thomas Cook**, www.thomasexchangeglobal.co.uk, or transferred via a bank draft, but this can take up to a week.

Cost of travelling

The Highlands and Islands of Scotland can be an expensive place to visit, and prices are higher in more remote parts, but there is plenty of budget accommodation available and backpackers will be able to keep their costs down. Petrol is a major expense and won't just cost an arm and a leg but also the limbs of all remaining family members. Expect to pay up to 15p per litre more than in central and southern parts of Scotland and don't pass a fuel station in the Highlands and Islands if short of fuel. Accommodation and restaurant prices also tend to be higher in more popular destinations and during the busy summer months.

The minimum daily budget required, if you're staying in hostels, very cheap B&Bs or camping, cycling or hitching (not recommended), and cooking your own meals, will be around £25-30 per person per day. If you start using public transport and eating out occasionally that will rise to around £35-40. Those staying in slightly more upmarket B&Bs or guesthouses, eating out every evening at pubs or modest restaurants and visiting tourist attractions, such as castles or museums, can expect to pay around £50-60 per day. If you also want to hire a car and use ferries to visit the islands, and eat well, then costs will rise considerably and you'll be looking at least £75-80 per person per day. Single travellers will have to pay more than ½ the cost of a double room in most places, and should budget on spending around 60-70% of what a couple would spend.

Opening hours

Businesses are usually open Mon-Sat 0900-1700. In towns and cities, as well as villages in holiday areas, many shops open on a Sun but they will open later and close earlier (for further details, see page 32). For TIC opening hours, see page 23. Those visiting the Outer Hebrides need to be aware of the strict observance of the Sabbath on those islands.

Post

Most post offices are open Mon-Fri 0900 to 1730 and Sat 0900-1230 or 1300. Smaller sub-post offices are closed for an hour at lunch (1300-1400) and many of them operate out of a shop. Post offices keep the same ½-day closing times as shops.

Stamps can be bought at post offices, but also from vending machines outside, and also at many newsagents. A 1st-class letter weighing up to 100 g to anywhere in the UK costs 36p and should arrive the following day, while 2nd-class letters weighing up to 100 g cost 27p and take between 2-4 days. For more information about Royal Mail postal services, call T08457-740740, or visit www.royalmail.com.

Safety

Incidences of serious crime in Highlands and Islands tend to be the exception rather than the rule and are so rare that they always make front page news. In fact, if someone failed to say 'good morning' – heaven forfend – it would provoke such an outrage that locals would be talking about little else for weeks to come. In most island communities, even sizeable ones such as Tobermory on Mull, people don't even lock their doors at night, and will even leave their car keys still in the lock. The major safety issue when visiting the Highlands and more remote parts relates to the unpredictable weather conditions. Everyone should be aware of the need for caution and proper preparation when walking or climbing in the mountains. For more information on mountain safety, see www.mountaineering-scotland.org.uk/safety.

Telephone → Country code +44.

Useful numbers: operator T100; international operator T155; directory enquiries T192; overseas directory enquiries T153.

Most public payphones are operated by **British Telecom (BT)** and can be found in towns and cities, though less so in rural areas. Numbers of public phone booths have declined in recent years due to the advent of the mobile phone, so don't rely on being able to find a payphone wherever you go. BT payphones take either coins (20p, 50p and £1) or phonecards, which are available at newsagents and post offices displaying the BT logo. These cards come in denominations of £2, £3, £5 and £10. Some payphones also accept credit cards.

For most countries (including Europe, USA and Canada) calls are cheapest Mon-Fri between 1800 and 0800 and all day Sat-Sun. For Australia and New Zealand it's cheapest to call from 1430-1930 and from 2400-0700 every day. Area codes are not needed if calling from within the same area. Any number prefixed by 0800 or 0500 is free to the caller; 08457 numbers are charged at local rates and 08705 numbers at the national rate. To call Scotland from overseas, dial 011 from USA and Canada, 0011 from Australia and 00 from New Zealand, followed by 44, then the area code, minus the first zero, then the number. To call overseas from Scotland dial 00 followed by the country code. Country codes include: Australia 61; Ireland 353; New Zealand 64; South Africa 27; USA and Canada 1.

Time

Greenwich Mean Time (GMT) is used from late Oct to late Mar, after which time the clocks go forward an hour to British Summer Time (BST). GMT is 5 hrs ahead of US Eastern Standard Time and 10 hrs behind Australian Eastern Standard Time.

Tipping

Believe it or not, people in Scotland do leave tips. In a restaurant you should leave a tip of 10-15% if you are satisfied with the service. If the bill already includes a service charge, you needn't add a further tip. Tipping is not normal in pubs or bars. Taxi drivers will expect a tip for longer journeys, usually of around 10%; and most hairdressers will also expect a tip. As in most other countries, porters, bellboys and waiters in more up-market hotels rely on tips to supplement their meagre wages.

Tourist information
Tourist Information Centres
Tourist offices – called tourist information centres (TICs) – can be found in most Scottish towns. Their addresses, phone numbers and opening hours are listed in the relevant sections of this book. Opening hours vary depending on the time of year, and many of the smaller offices are closed during the winter months. All tourist offices provide information on accommodation, public transport, local attractions and restaurants, as well as selling books, local guides, maps and souvenirs. Many also have free street plans and leaflets describing local walks. They can also book accommodation for you, for a small fee.

Museums, galleries and historic houses
Most of Scotland's tourist attractions, apart from the large museums and art galleries in the main cities, are open only from Easter-Oct. Full details of opening hours and admission charges are given in the relevant sections of this guide.

Over 100 of the country's most prestigious sights, and 75,000 ha of beautiful countryside, are cared for by the **National Trust for Scotland** (NTS), 26-31 Charlotte Sq, Edinburgh EH2 4ET, T0844-493 2100, www.nts.org.uk. National Trust properties are indicated in this guide as 'NTS', and entry charges and opening hours are given for each property.

Historic Scotland (HS), Longmore House, Salisbury Pl, Edinburgh EH9 1SH, T0131-668 8600, www.historic-scotland.gov.uk, manages more than 330 of Scotland's most important castles, monuments and other historic sites. Historic Scotland properties are indicated as 'HS', and admission charges and opening hours are also given in this guide. Historic Scotland offers an Explorer Pass which allows free entry to 70 of its properties including Edinburgh and Stirling castles. A 3-day pass (can be used over 5 consecutive days) costs £25, concessions £20, family £50, 7-day pass (valid for 14 days) £34, £27, £68. It can save a lot of money, especially in Orkney, where most of the monuments are managed by Historic Scotland.

Many other historic buildings are owned by local authorities, and admission is cheap, or in many cases free. Most fee-paying attractions give a discount or concession for senior citizens, the unemployed, full-time students and children under 16 (those under 5 are admitted free everywhere). Proof of age or status must be shown. Many of Scotland's stately homes are still owned and occupied by the landed gentry, and admission is usually between £4 and £8.

Finding out more
The best way of finding out more information for your trip to Scotland is to contact Visit Scotland (aka the Scottish Tourist Board), www.visitbritain.com. Alternatively, you can contact VisitBritain, the organization that is responsible for tourism throughout the British Isles. Both organizations can provide a wealth of free literature and information such as maps, city guides and accommodation brochures. If particularly interested in ensuring your visit coincides with a major festival or sporting event, it's also worthwhile having a look at EventScotland's website, www.eventscotland.org. Travellers with special needs should also contact Visit- Scotland or their nearest VisitBritain office. If you want more detailed information on a particular area, contact the specific tourist boards, see below.

VisitScotland regional offices

Orkney Tourist Board, 6 Broad St, Kirkwall, Orkney KW15 1NX, T01856-872001, www.visitorkney.com.

Visit Shetland, Market Cross, Lerwick, Shetland ZE1 0LU, T08701-999440, www.visitshetland.com.

Visas and immigration

Visa regulations are subject to change, so it is essential to check with your local British embassy, high commission or consulate before leaving home. Citizens of all European countries – except Albania, Bosnia Herzegovina, Kosovo, Macedonia, Moldova, Turkey, Serbia and all former Soviet republics (other than the Baltic states) – require only a passport to enter Britain and can generally stay for up to 3 months. Citizens of Australia, Canada, New Zealand, South Africa or the USA can stay for up to 6 months, providing they have a return ticket and sufficient funds to cover their stay. Citizens of most other countries require a visa from the commission or consular office in the country of application.

The **Foreign and Commonwealth Office** (FCO), T0207-270 1500, www.fco.gov.uk, has an excellent website, which provides details of British immigration and visa requirements. Also the Home Office UK Border Agency is responsible for UK immigration matters and its website is a good place to start for anyone hoping visit, work, study or emigrate to the UK. Call the immigration enquiry bureau on T0870-6067 766 or visit www.bia.homeoffice.gov.uk.

For visa extensions also contact the **Home Office UK Border Agency** via the above number or its website. The agency can also be reached at Lunar House, Wellesley Rd, Croydon, London CR9. Citizens of Australia, Canada, New Zealand, South Africa or the USA wishing to stay longer than 6 months will need an Entry Clearance Certificate from the British High Commission in their country. For more details, contact your nearest British embassy, consulate or high commission, or the Foreign and Commonwealth Office in London.

Weights and measures

Imperial and metric systems are both in use. Distances on roads are measured in miles and yards, drinks poured in pints and gills, but generally, the metric system is used elsewhere.

Volunteering

See www.volunteerscotland.org.uk.
The British Trust for Conservation Volunteers, Sedum House, Mallard Way, Doncaster DN4 8DB, T01302-388883, www.btcv.org. Get fit in the 'green gym', planting hedges, creating wildlife gardens or improving footpaths.
Earthwatch, 57 Woodstock Rd, Oxford OX2 6HJ, T01865-318838. Team up with scientists studying our furry friends.
Jubilee Sailing Trust, Hazel Rd, Southampton, T023-804 9108, www.jst. org.uk. Work on deck on an adventure holiday.
National Trust for Scotland, Wemyss House, 28 Charlotte Sq, Edinburgh EH2 4ET, T0844-493 2100, www.nts.org.uk. Among a number of Scotland based charities that offer volunteering opportunities. You could find yourself helping restore buildings on St Kilda or taking part in an archaeological dig on Loch Lomondside.

Contents

Footprint features

Skye & the Small Isles

Isle of Skye

The Isle of Skye (An t-Eilean Sgitheanach) gets its name from the Norse word for cloud (skuy) and is commonly known as Eilean a Cheo (the Misty Isle), so it obviously rains a lot here. But when the rain stops and the mist clears, the views make the heart soar. There are the surreal rock formations of the Trotternish Peninsula, the hummocky strangeness of Fairy Glen and the gentler pleasures of Sleat in the south. And then there are the Cuillins. Certainly, Skye is one of the best places in Scotland for outdoor types: it offers air, sea, land and light in their purest form and any visitor will return home physically refreshed and spiritually uplifted. Aside from swooning at the island's natural beauty, the most popular destination is Dunvegan Castle, stronghold of the Macleod clan, while their old enemies, the MacDonalds hail from the Sleat Peninsula in the south of the island. The most famous Macdonald, Flora, who helped Bonnie Prince Charles flee to France, was born at Milton on South Uist but latterly moved to Skye and was buried at Kilmuir in 1790. ⇒ *For listings, see pages 40-47.*

Ins and outs

Getting there
The quickest route to Skye is across the bridge (no toll) from Kyle of Lochalsh to Kyleakin. Coach services run to Skye from Glasgow (via Fort William) and Inverness (bus No 917), with connections to all main cities in the UK (**Scottish Citylink**, T0871-266 3333; **National Express**, T0871-781 8178). The Citylink bus service from Inverness runs three times daily and the journey takes three to four hours. The Glasgow service runs to Kyleakin, Portree and Uig, three to four times daily and it takes three hours to reach Portree from Fort William. Winter services are less frequent with only a few buses in each direction each day.
There is also a train service from Kyle of Lochalsh to Inverness, see page 255. Eyed from the south, the high arch of Skye Bridge is certainly dramatic. A still more scenic approach to the island is by ferry from Mallaig to Armadale, on the southern Sleat Peninsula. The car and passenger ferry makes this 30-minute crossing eight times each way Monday to Saturday, and six times on Sunday (reduced sailings in winter). Booking is recommended, call T08000-665000 or visit www.calmac.co.uk. The one-way trip costs £4.05 per passenger and £21.20 per car. A five-day saver return is £6.80 and £36.50. Trains from Fort William and Glasgow Queen Street connect with some of the ferries, see www.firstscotrail.co.uk.

The best way to Skye is from Glenelg to Kylerhea, south of Kyleakin. The tiny community-owned car ferry makes the 10-minute crossing every 20 minutes, daily from Easter to October between 1000 and 1800. Between June and the end of August it sails until 1900. The cost per car is £12 or £15 return (with up to four passengers), see page 255 for details. Information and ticket bookings can be found at www.skyeferry.co.uk. ➡ *For further details, see Transport page 47.*

Getting around

Skye is the second largest Hebridean island (after Harris and Lewis), at almost 50 miles long and between seven and 25 miles wide. It is possible to run up a hefty mileage as the extensive road system penetrates to all but the most remote corners of its many peninsulas. It is possible to get around by public transport midweek, with postbuses supplementing the normal services, but, as everywhere in the Highlands and Islands, buses are few and far between at weekends, especially Sunday, and during the winter. Buses run between Portree, Broadford, Uig (for ferries to the Western Isles), Kyleakin, Armadale (for ferries to Mallaig), Dunvegan and Carbost, and a more limited service runs from Broadford to Elgol and Portree to Glen Brittle. Getting around by public transport is more time consuming in winter (October to March) as bus services are less frequent on some routes. ➡ *For further details, see Activities and tours page 46, and Transport page 47.*

Tourist information

Skye is well served by all types of accommodation: B&Bs, guesthouses, hostels, bunk-houses, campsites and some very fine hotels. During the peak summer months advance bookings are recommended. These can be made directly or through the island's tourist information centres in Portree, Broadford, Uig and Dunvegan. See www.visithighlands.com, and www.isleofskye.com. For local tourist information centres see individual sections.

Portree → *For listings, see pages 40-47. Phone code 01478.*

Portree is Skye's capital and, as such, is a functional kind of place with all the attendant facilities and services you'd expect to find in the island's main settlement. That said, it's fairly attractive; a busy fishing port built around a natural harbour, with a row of brightly painted houses along the shorefront and the rest of the town rising steeply up to the central , the centre of which is now dominated by a public car park (pay and display).

Ins and outs

Getting there and around Portree is ideally placed for trips to all but the most south-westerly parts of the island. Buses leave from the bus station in Somerled Square to Dunvegan, Uig, Broadford, Kyleakin, Armadale, the Talisker Distillery and Glenbrittle. There are also services to the mainland. The town is compact enough to get around easily on foot, though there is a regular town bus service for those needing to get into the centre from the outskirts.

Tourist information The helpful **TIC** ⓘ *Bayfield Rd, T01478-612137, year-round Mon-Sat,* has bus timetables, a good selection of books and maps, internet access and several (20p) leaflets outlining local walking routes including the 2-mile-long Portree Forest walk.

Sights

Aros Experience ① *Viewfield Rd, ½ a mile from town centre on the road to Broadford, T01478-613649, www.aros.co.uk, Easter-Oct daily 0900-1800, Nov-Dec daily 0900-1730, £4.50, concessions £3.50, children under 12 free*, provides a 20 minute audio-visual display of the island's history and cultural heritage, and a birds-eye 'live cam' view of a sea eagles nest. The island's only theatre is housed here and features a varied programme of events, including drama, traditional music, comedy and films (see Entertainment, page 45). There's also a restaurant with reasonable snacks and a shop selling tartan souvenirs, which seems to dominate the Aros experience. Certainly, culturally this place is no replacement for the much missed An Tuireann Arts Centre further up the road which closed in 2008 after failing to satisfy the bean counters.

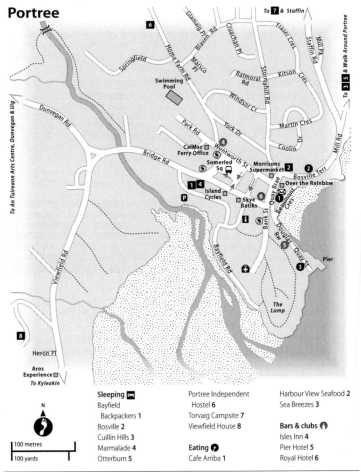

Portree

Sleeping 🛏	Portree Independent	Harbour View Seafood **2**
Bayfield	Hostel **6**	Sea Breezes **3**
Backpackers **1**	Torvaig Campsite **7**	
Bosville **2**	Viewfield House **8**	Bars & clubs 🎶
Cuillin Hills **3**		Isles Inn **4**
Marmalade **4**	Eating 🍴	Pier Hotel **5**
Otterburn **5**	Cafe Arriba **1**	Royal Hotel **6**

A nice, gentle introduction to walking in the area, and an opportunity to stretch your legs before tackling more strenuous routes such as the Old Man of Storr or the Quiraing, starts out from Bosville Terrace. Follow the street as it curves round, then take the right fork at the first junction, down towards the shore. Just after the car park to the right the road splits: follow the path to the right along the northern shore of the bay. The path follows the shore and passes a viewpoint and flagpole. It then becomes rougher as it swings round the headland and reaches a gate in a dyke. Go through the gate and cross the muddy field, then follow the fence up to the left until you reach another gate. Climb over the gate and continue along the edge of the next field, then cross a stile at the top. Walk up the slope to the clear track and follow this left as it heads uphill. You'll then see some houses; take the track beyond the house on the left and follow it down between two large farm buildings. The path heads down across rough moorland towards Portree. Cross the stile and continue downhill through some woods; then you'll see a hotel on your left before rejoining the original road near the car park. It's about two and a half miles and takes about one and a half hours at an easy pace. The path can get very muddy in places. Details of several local walks can be found in the TIC.

Trotternish Peninsula → *For listings, see pages 40-47. Phone code 01470.*

North from Portree is the 30-mile-long Trotternish Peninsula, sticking out like a giant thumb hitching a lift from a passing ferry. The interior of the peninsula is a basaltic lava wilderness full of bizarre rock formations. A 20-mile-long escarpment of sheer cliffs and towering pinnacles dominates the landscape. The best known of these strange formations, the **Quiraing** and **Old Man of Storr**, can be explored on foot (see below and page 31). The A855 and A87 roads follow the coast around the peninsula, and a spectacular minor road bisects the ridge from Staffin Bay to Uig. Trotternish is best explored with your own transport, but there are a few daily buses covering the circular route from Portree.

Uig
The A87 runs northwest from Portree to the tiny ferry port of Uig, dramatically set in a horseshoe bay and the departure point for ferries to **Tarbert** (Harris) and **Lochmaddy** (North Uist). The island's busy and helpful **Caledonian MacBrayne** ① *T0800-665000, www.calmac.co.uk*, ferry booking office is here whilst just 20 yds past CalMac's door you'll also find the production nerve centre (and shop) of the acclaimed **Skye Brewery** ① *T01470-542477, www.skyebrewery. co.uk*, which exports its ales around the world. Alternatively, also by the CalMac office, kids will enjoy painting their own earthenware pot at the **Uig Pottery** ① *May-Sep Mon-Sat.*

Just outside the village is the magical **Fairy Glen**. Turn right just before the **Uig Hotel** coming down the hill from the Portree direction. About a mile up the single track road you enter an eerie, mysterious world of perfect conical hills, some up to 60-ft high. It's almost inconceivable that these are natural formations, and the inevitable mist only adds to the spooky strangeness of the place.

Uig to Duntulm
At **Kilmuir** is the **Skye Museum of Island Life** ① *T01470-552206, Easter-Oct Mon-Sat 0930-1700, £2.50, children £2*. The group of thatched houses give a fascinating insight into a crofting community's way of life of at the end of the 19th century, and is the most authentic of several such museums on Skye. Behind the museum, at the end of the road, is **Flora MacDonald's Monument**, which marks the grave of Skye's most famous daughter, with her husband buried alongside. The rather austere memorial is inscribed with Dr

Take no prisoners

Violent conflict between neighbouring clan chiefs was so commonplace on Skye and in the rest of the Western Highlands that it was almost accepted as part of the very fabric of society. One particularly gruesome example took place on Eigg in 1577. The Macleods had taken refuge in a cave but their presence was discovered by the MacDonalds, who piled brushwood at the entrance and set fire to it, burning alive the 395 people sheltering inside, almost the entire population of the island. Revenge came the following year, at Trumpan church in Ardmore Bay on Skye. The Macleods landed under cover of the early morning fog and set light to the church, burning the congregation inside.

Johnson's poignant tribute, see box, page 31. Indeed, so highly regarded was 'Flory' that it's said her funeral was the largest ever seen in the Highlands. Apparently, her cortege stretched for 1½ miles whilst over 300 gallons of whisky were drunk at her wake!

At the northwest tip of the peninsula, 15 minutes' drive from Uig, is **Duntulm Castle**, a dramatic ruin perched atop a steep cliff, haunted by keening winds and the ghosts of its tragic past: according to local legend, the castle was abandoned around 1732 when a nursemaid accidentally let the baby heir fall from a window onto the cliffs below. The 15th-century structure, built on the site of an ancient Norse stronghold, became the chief Skye residence of the powerful MacDonalds and was the most imposing castle in the Hebrides.

The Quiraing walk

Beyond Duntulm the A855 heads across the tip of the peninsula to the east coast, where the famous bizarre rock scenery is found. At the north end of **Staffin Bay**, a minor road cuts across the peninsula to Uig. This road is the access point for the Quiraing, the famous jumble of strangely shaped hills and rocks that is one of the island's classic walks. This four-mile walk is quite demanding, but the dramatic scenery more than compensates. To get to the starting point, drive 19 miles north from Portree on the A855. At Brogaig, just north of Staffin, take the single-track road to Uig. Follow it and, just after the road has zigzagged its way up the face of the ridge, park in the car park to the left. Cross the road and follow the well-defined path along the base of the cliffs, with a steep grassy slope down to the right. After about one mile you'll start to see some of the well-known rocky features on the far side of a rough valley. The most imposing of these is **The Prison**, a huge, tilted square block. On the left, among the towering cliffs, is **The Needle**, a shaft of rock about 120-ft high. Scramble up the narrow gully to the left of The Needle to reach **The Table**, an area of flat grassland surrounded by high cliffs (local shinty teams used to play here). From The Table continue along the path at the foot of the cliffs, past a small lochan on the right and through a stone dyke, until you reach the lowest point of the ridge on your left. Scramble up on to the ridge and make your way back along the tops of the cliffs (take care at this point). There's a hard climb up the slopes of Meall na Suirmamach, but the views from the top are spectacular. Continue along the top of the cliffs for just over a mile and you'll see the car park. Even if you don't attempt the walk, the road over the back of the Trotternish ridge from Uig makes a worthwhile detour.

Kilt Rock

A few miles south of Staffin Bay is Kilt Rock, an impressive 60-m sea cliff which gets its name from the vertical columnar basalt strata overlying horizontal ones beneath. A rather

Faithful Flora

In Kilmuir graveyard is the memorial which marks the grave of Flora MacDonald, one of the most famous characters in Skye's long history. The memorial bears Dr Johnson's fitting epitaph: A name that will be mentioned in history, and if courage and fidelity be virtues, mentioned with honour.

It was Flora MacDonald who helped Bonnie Prince Charlie to escape capture following the Jacobite defeat at Culloden in 1746. Pursued by government troops, the prince fled from South Uist 'over the sea to Skye' aboard Flora's boat, disguised as an Irish servant girl by the name of

Betty Burke. He then made his way to Portree, where he bade farewell to the young woman who had risked her own life to protect him.

When Flora's part in the prince's escape became known, she was immediately arrested and sent to the Tower of London. She was released a year later, married a Skye man and then emigrated to North Carolina where she spent the next 12 years of her life. They returned to her husband's house in Kingsburgh in 1786. Flora died in Skye in 1790, and it is said that her funeral was the largest ever witnessed in the Highlands.

---

tenuous comparison perhaps, but the cliffs south of Staffin are particularly spectacular, as are the **Lealt Falls**, a torrent of mountain water at the head of a gorge, a few miles south of Kilt Rock. The falls are signposted by the road, so all you have to do is park the car and peer over. Just before the turn for Kilt Rock at Ellishadder is the wee **Staffin Museum** ① *May-Oct*, sporting such finds as a dinosaur bone and Bronze Age artefacts.

Old Man of Storr walk

A few miles further south, and seven miles north of Portree, is a car park which is the starting point for another of Skye's famous walks: up to the Old Man of Storr, the distinctive pinnacle which has detached itself from the cliffs of the Storr behind. This basalt finger of rock, 165 ft high, stands beneath the steep cliffs of **The Storr** (2360 ft) and is visible from the A855. The starting point for the three and a half mile walk up and back (1½ hours) is the car park on the left, just over six miles north of Portree, near the northern end of Loch Leathan, which can be reached by bus from Portree. Cross the stile over the wall by the Forestry Commission sign and follow the clear track up through the conifer plantation. The track is a gradual uphill climb until you come out into open grassland. Go through the gate in the fence and then it's a steep climb up the grassy slope with the massive pinnacle towering overhead. Once at the top you enter an area of weird and impressive rock formations. You can follow any of the dozens of paths that lead between the rocks, or just enjoy the fantastic views across to Raasay and the mainland beyond. You can follow the same path back down to the car park.

Waternish, Dunvegan and Duirinish

→ *For listings, see pages 40-47. Phone code 01470.*

In the northwest of Skye the peninsulas of Waternish (or Vaternish) and Duirinish point out into the Minch towards the Western Isles. The larger Duirinish Peninsula holds more interest for the visitor, featuring the beautiful green valley of **Glendale**, an area brimming with history, the dramatic walk to **Neist Point** and **Dunvegan Castle**, Skye's most famous landmark.

Things to do on Skye when it's raining

Just in case you didn't know, it can rain quite often on Skye and, unless you're one of those hardy souls who's prepared to brave the elements, you'll need to know about the island's main indoor attractions. There are numerous opportunities to shelter from the rain, but most of them cost money and many will leave you regretting it, so here's our list of the top 10 things to do. Details of opening times and admission prices are given under each relevant destination.

Beginning in Portree, there's the **Aros Experience** (page 28), which gives a good introduction to the island's history. North of Uig, at Kilmuir on the Trotternish Peninsula, is the **Skye Museum of Island Life** (page 29), which pretty much does what it says on the sign. Northwest from Portree is **Dunvegan Castle** (see below), home of the Clan Macleod and top of most visitors' itineraries. On the road to Dunvegan is **Edinbane Pottery** (page 32), where you can buy pots of every shape and size and watch them being made.

Travelling south from Dunvegan, you'll reach the turn-off to the **Talisker Distillery** (page 35), the island's only whisky distillery, where you can sample the distinctive peaty taste. While you're there you can visit nearby **Carbostcraft Pottery** (page 45), in the village of Carbost, and indulge in some more gift buying. If you're in need of some refreshment after all that culture and shopping, you could do a lot worse than the bar at the **Sligachan Hotel** (page 44), which boasts an impressive array of whiskies and climbers' beards. In the southern peninsula of Sleat, near the Armadale ferry terminal, is **Armadale Castle** (page 39), with a visitor centre that is worth visiting. Nearby is one of the branches of **Skye Batiks** (page 46), with a huge selection of these 'new age' style fabrics in a range of original Celtic designs (the other branch is in Portree). And for that final drink before boarding the ferry to Mallaig, pop into the cosy bar of the **Hotel Eilean Iarmain** (page 46), which serves wonderful food.

Edinbane

The turn-off to this much-visited part of the island is four miles northwest of Portree. The A850 swings west towards Dunvegan but eight miles before the castle and at the head of Loch Greshornish is the tiny village of Edinbane, where there's a campsite, two hotels, several B&Bs, a petrol station and the renowned **Edinbane Pottery** ① *T01470-582234, www.edinbane-pottery.co.uk, 0900-1800 Nov-Easter weekdays and Easter-Oct daily. workshop and showroom*, which is a must for hunters of imaginative hand-crafted souvenirs.

Waternish Peninsula

The A850 continues west. Those with their own transport and time on their hands might wish to make an interesting little detour at the **Fairy Bridge**, where the B886 runs north to **Trumpan**, near the tip of the Waternish Peninsula. If the weather's good (and it is, occasionally), this is the best place to watch the sun set in a blaze of red over the Outer Hebrides. If there's no sunset, then you could always visit **Skyeskyns** ① *T01470-592237, www.skyeskyns.co.uk, daily 0900-1800*, in Loch Bay, the country's only traditional exhibition tannery. While here, you could also pop into the island's oldest pub, the **Stein Inn** (see Sleeping, page 45). Close by, you can buy high quality handspun Scottish merino wools and cashmere at **Shilasdair** ① *T01470-592297, daily 1000-1800*.

The ruined church at Trumpan, at the end of the road, has some grisly skeletons in its cupboard (see box on page 30). In the graveyard is the 'trial stone'. A hole in the stone was used to test whether or not an accused person was telling the truth. If they could quickly find the hole and stick their arm through it while blindfolded, they were found innocent, but if not, they were guilty. The church is also the starting point for the strenuous 8-mile walk out to **Waternish point** and back.

Dunvegan

A few miles further on from the turn-off to Waternish is the little village of Dunvegan. Just to the north of the village is proud **Dunvegan Castle** ① *T01470-521206, www.dunvegan castle.com, Apr-mid Oct daily 1000-1730, mid Oct -Apr daily 1100-1600, castle and gardens £9, concessions £7, children £4.50, gardens only £7, concessions £6, children £3.50,* the island's most important tourist attraction. The no. 56 Stagecoach bus serves the castle, running from Glendale to Portree via Dunvegan, and back

The castle is the home of the chiefs of the Clan Macleod who have lived here for over seven centuries, making it the oldest continuously inhabited castle in Britain. The present structure dates from the 15th and 16th centuries and, though the Victorian restoration has left it looking more like a baronial house, a look inside reveals its true age. Among the few genuinely interesting relics on display is Rory Mor's horn, a huge drinking vessel which the chief's heir must drain 'without setting down or falling down', when filled with claret (about one and a half bottles). There's also a lock of Bonnie Prince Charlie's hair, clipped from his head by Flora MacDonald as a keepsake, but pride of place goes to the Fairy Flag. The flag has been dated to between the fourth and seventh centuries and is made of Middle Eastern silk. It is said to have been given to the clan chief by a fairy, and has the power to ensure victory in battle for the clan on three occasions. It has been used twice so far. The lovely castle gardens lead down to the lochside jetty, from where you can take a **seal-spotting cruise** ① *T01470-521500, May-Oct daily, £7, children £4.* These shores are reportedly inhabited by 35% of Skye's seal population. Nevertheless, you'll get a refund if you fail to spot one. There's also a busy restaurant and gift shop by the castle gates.

In the village of Dunvegan is **Giant Angus MacAskill Museum** ① *T01470-521296, Easter-Oct daily 0930-1800, £1.50, concessions £1, children free,* housed in a thatched, whitewashed cottage, which relates the life story of the tallest ever Scotsman, Angus MacAskill, born on the Outer Hebridean island of Berneray and who grew to 7 ft 9 ins tall. He emigrated to Novia Scotia and toured the United States with the midget General Tom Thumb, who is said to have danced on his outstretched hand. More interesting than the museum though, are the stories of its owner, Peter MacAskill, in particular the one about the replica coffin, which is worth the admission fee alone. Peter is a descendent of Angus and also runs the museum at Colbost (see below).

Duirinish Peninsula

West of Dunvegan is the Duirinish Peninsula. The northern half is populated along the western shores of **Loch Dunvegan** and in the beautiful and green **Glendale**, an area brimming with history but with hardly an island family left. Glendale is now dubbed 'Little England', owing to the large number of incoming settlers from the south. The area is famed throughout the Highlands and Islands, for it was here in 1882 that local crofters, spurred on by the **Battle of the Braes**, see box, page 35, resisted the cruel and petty tyranny of their estate manager. The authorities sent a gunboat to deal with the uprising and arrested the ringleaders, some of whom were imprisoned in Edinburgh and became known as the 'Glendale Martyrs'. This episode sparked a radical movement throughout the Highlands and led to the Crofter's Holdings Act of 1886, which gave the crofters a more secure tenure and fair rent. The uninhabited southern half of the peninsula is dominated by Healabhal Bheag (1601 ft) and Healabhal Mhor (1538 ft), a pair of decapitated hills known as **Macleod's Tables**. They are so named because legend has it that the clan chief held a huge open-air feast for King James V on one of the hilltops.

The **Glendale Visitor Route** is signposted from just before Dunvegan village and leads westwards along the shores of the loch and across the peninsula. There are several interesting little sights along the way. Those interested in finding out more about the region's history, and crofting on the island, should head for the **Colbost Folk Museum** ① *T01470-521296, Easter-Oct daily 0930-1800, £1.50, concessions £1, children free*, housed in a restored blackhouse, with a peat fire burning and an illicit still out the back. The museum is adjacent to the **Three Chimneys** restaurant and four miles from Dunvegan on the B884 to Glendale. A little further on is **Skye Silver** ① *T01470-511263, Mar-Oct daily 1000-1800*, where you can buy silver jewellery in traditional Celtic designs. Further north is the studio of **Diana Mackie** ① *T01470-511795 (phone for appointment), www.diana-mackie.co.uk*, who designed the interior of the renowned Three Chimneys restaurant (see above) and whose landscape artwork is inspired by the dramatic coastal scenery just beyond her door.

Borreraig was home to the famous MacCrimmons, hereditary pipers to the Macleod chiefs and the first composers, players and teachers of *piobaireachd* (pibroch), which can be heard at an annual recital at Dunvegan Castle in early August. The ruins of the ancient piping college can still be seen. Moving from the sublime to the ridiculous, in the village of **Glendale** is a **Toy Museum** ① *T01470-511240, www.toy-museum.co.uk, all year Mon-Sat 1000-1800, £3, concessions £2, children £1*, which should appeal to kids of all ages.

The B884 continues west, then a road turns off left for Waterstein. At the end of this road (just over two miles) is a car park which is the starting point for the walk out to the lighthouse at **Neist Point**, the most westerly point on Skye and one of the most pleasant walks on the island. It's about 1½ miles there and back and well worth the effort. The path is easy to follow and the views of the sea cliffs are wonderful. There are lots of nesting seabirds around and you might even spot whales offshore. The **lighthouse**, built in 1909, is now unmanned.

The Cuillins and Minginish

→ *For listings, see pages 40-47. OS Landranger No 32 & OS Outdoor Leisure No 8.*

The district of Minginish is the wildest and least-populated part of the island, but for many it is the greatest attraction, for this is where the Cuillins are to be found. This hugely impressive mountain range, often shrouded in rain or cloud, is the spiritual heartland of the island and, when it's clear their heart-aching grandeur can be appreciated from every other peninsula on Skye. Though officially called the Cuillin 'Hills', these present some of the toughest climbing in Britain. Indeed, the magnificent scenery and vast range of (high and low level) walks and scrambles have attracted climbers and walkers for centuries, but have also claimed many lives. It cannot be stressed too strongly that the Cuillin ridge, whilst famous and spectacular is also an exposed and demanding route that should only be attempted by experienced climbers and/or with a qualified guide. For further information, see page 26.

Walks into the Cuillins

There are three routes into the Cuillins: from the Sligachan Hotel, from Glen Brittle, and from Elgol. The eastern part of the range is known as the **Red Cuillins**. Their smoother,

Law of the land

One of the most significant incidents in the island's history took place in April 1882, when a group of around 100 local crofters and their families fought a pitched battle against a force of 60 police sent by the government from Glasgow. The 'Battle of the Braes', as it became known, was caused, like many other such uprisings throughout the Highlands and Islands, by threatened evictions. The local crofters were so incensed by the injustice of the eviction notices served on them that they destroyed the offending documents, leading the government to dispatch its police force. The defeat of the government forces of law and order by a bunch of men, women and children with sticks and stones is often described as the last battle fought on British soil, and led eventually to the establishment of a Royal Commission to look into the crofters' grievances.

conical granite peaks contrast sharply with the older, darker gabbro of the jagged-edged **Black Cuillins** to the west. The latter are particularly suitable for rock climbing and best approached from Glen Brittle, while the former are accessed from the Sligachan Hotel. There are 20 'Munros' (mountains over 3000 ft in height) in the Cuillins, with the highest being Sgurr Alasdair, at 3251 ft. Though the sheer majesty of the mountains can only be appreciated at close quarters by the climber, there are impressive views from Elgol, from the road into Glen Brittle and, more distantly, from the west coast of Sleat. **Glen Sligachan** is one of the most popular routes into the Cuillin range and the main access point for the more forgiving Red Cuillins, the walk to **Loch Coruisk**, or the ascent of **Marsco**.

Glen Brittle → *Phone code 01478.*

Six miles along the A863 to Dunvegan from Sligachan is a turning left to Portnalong, Carbost and the Talisker Distillery (see below), which soon leads to the entrance to Glen Brittle. To reach Glen Brittle, take the Portree–Carbost–Fiscavaig bus (Stagecoach No 53/54). Get off at the turn-off and then walk the remaining 8 miles.

The road down Glen Brittle affords great views of the western side of the imposing Black Cuillins, until it ends at the campsite and shore at the foot of the glen. From Glen Brittle there are numerous paths leading up to the corries of the Black Cuillins. There are many alternative options for those wishing to continue up to the upper corries or to the main ridge. One of the finest of the Cuillin corries is **Coire Lagan**. This walk starts from the beach at Glen Brittle village and takes you up to the lochan in the upper coire, with Sgurr Alasdair, the most difficult of the Munros, towering overhead. A fine Cuillin sampler is the short walk to the spectacular **Eas Mor** waterfall.

Talisker → *Phone code 01478.*

A recommended trip for whisky drinkers, or if it's raining, is to the excellent **Talisker Distillery** ① *T01478-614308, www.discovering-distilleries.com, Apr-Oct Mon-Sat 0930-1700, Jul-Aug daily 1100-1700, Nov-Mar Mon-Fri 1000-1700, tours, £5,* at **Carbost** on the shores of Loch Harport, on the B8009 (not in the village of Talisker itself, which is on the west coast). This is Skye's only whisky distillery and produces a very smoky, peaty single malt, with a distinctive hot, peppery palate, particularly the 20- and 25-year-old expressions. The entry fee includes a discount voucher on any 70cl bottle of malt whisky sold in the shop.

Elgol → *Phone code 01471.*

One of the most rewarding drives on Skye is the 14-mile single-track road from Broadford to Elgol (Ealaghol), a tiny settlement near the tip of the Strathaird Peninsula, from where you can enjoy the classic view of the Cuillins from across Loch Scavaig and also see the islands of Soay, Rùm and Canna. It was from here, on 4 July 1746, that the Young Pretender finally left the Hebrides. Before leaving, he was given a farewell banquet by the MacKinnons in what is now called **Prince Charlie's Cave**. There's also the added attraction of a dramatic boat trip, to the mouth of **Loch Coruisk**, in the heart of the Black Cuillin. The glacial sea loch, romanticized by Walter Scott and painted by Turner, is over 2 miles long but only a few hundred yards wide, closed in by the sheer cliffs on either side and overshadowed by the towering mountains of black basalt and gabbro. The road to Elgol also gives great views of Bla Bheinn (pronounced Blaven), best seen from Torrin, at the head of Loch Slapin.

Elgol to Camasunary Bay

Elgol is the starting point for the walk to Camasunary Bay. This 9-mile coastal walk is quite demanding, but on a clear day the views of the Cuillins make it well worth the effort. It starts from the car park in Elgol. From here, walk back up the road for a short distance, then turn left along a track behind some houses, signposted for 'Garsbheinn'. Beside the last of these houses is a sign for the path to Coruisk. Follow this path along a steep grassy slope. The views across Loch Scavaig to the island of Soay and the Cuillins behind are marvellous. The slope gets even steeper beneath Ben Cleat, and you'll need a good head for heights to continue across the foot of Glen Scaladal, crossing a burn in the process (which can be tricky if it's in spate). Then it's on along the path beyond Beinn Leacach to Camasunary Bay, with its backdrop of mighty Sgurr na Stri and Bla Bheinn. The shortest way back is to retrace your steps but, as an alternative, follow the clear track from Camasunary up the right side of Abhainn nan Lean over the hills to the east until it joins the B8083 from Broadford. From here it's about three and a half miles back along the road to Elgol.

Broadford and the east coast → *For listings, see pages 40-47.*

Broadford (An t-Ath Leathann), Skye's second-largest village, basically consists of a mile-long main street strung out along a wide bay. The village may be low on charm but it's high on tourist facilities and makes a good base for exploring the south and east of the island. The road north from Broadford to Portree passes through Sconser, departure point for the short ferry ride to the little-visited island of Raasay.

Broadford

Broadford has plenty of accommodation and places to eat. Next to the Esso station is a Co-op, there's a laundrette in the petrol station shop (open 24 hours) and a bank with ATM. There is no tourist office as such, just an information point housed in the Otter Shop in the main car park (with erratic opening hours). Broadford is also home to one of the most incongruous attractions on the island, or elsewhere in the Highlands, the **Skye Serpentarium** ① *The Old Mill, Harrapool, T01471-822209, www.skyeserpentarium.org.uk, Apr-Oct Mon-Sat 1000-1700, Jul-Aug daily 1000-1700, £3.50, children £2,* a rescue centre for all kinds of snakes, lizards and other reptiles, which you can look at or touch: a welcome retreat if it's raining. Housed within the same rustic mill building is the cosy **Old Mill Café** ① *T01471-822800,* where you can feast on home-baking. Whilst just 50 m behind here is the fabulous **Creelers Restaurant** (see Eating, page 45).

Kyleakin

The opening of the Skye Bridge, linking the island with the Kyle of Lochalsh (see page 252), has turned the former ferry terminal of Kyleakin (Caol Acain) into a quiet backwater, though the absence of road traffic and coastal views north and across to Lochalsh make it a pleasant place to stay. It's particularly popular with backpackers. The bridge is supported in the middle on the small islet of **Eilean Ban**, erstwhile home of author and naturalist, Gavin Maxwell, and now home to an otter sanctuary. It can be visited as part of tour from the **Bright Water Visitor Centre** ① *Kyleakin, T01599-530040, www.eileanban.org, Apr-Oct Mon-Fri 1000-1700 (opening times vary so call ahead), free (donations welcome)*. The interactive centre is worth a visit, especially if you have kids, and the keepers cottages on Eilean Ban can be rented for between £300-570 per week, which is ideal for wildlife enthusiasts. In Kyleakin, by the pier, history buffs can read up about the ruin of **Castle Maol** on the headland and how in 1263 King Haakon once sailed into the area with 120 ships in preparation for doing battle with King Alexander III of Scotland. The village pub, **King Haakon**, serves good bar meals but if you'd prefer a curry, try the recently opened **Taste of India** ① *T01599-534134*, just past the roundabout on the road to Portree.

Kylerhea

About 4 miles out of Kyleakin a road turns left off the A87 and heads southeast to Kylerhea (pronounced Kile-ray). The bridge may be the most convenient route to Skye, but the best way to cross is on the small car and passenger ferry that makes the 10-minute crossing to Kylerhea from Glenelg. For full details of times and prices, see page 27. Near Kylerhea is the Forestry Commission **Otter Haven** ① *T01320-366322, daily 0900 till 1 hr before dusk, free*. An hour-long nature trail takes you to an observation hide where you can look out for these elusive creatures.

Broadford to Portree

The road north to Portree runs between the fringes of the Red Cuillins and the coast, giving good views across to the **Isle of Scalpay**.

Continuing north, the road then turns west past Luib and along the shores of brooding Loch Ainort until it reaches **Sconser**, the departure point for the ferry to Raasay and then climbs around Loch Sligachan before descending into Portree. On the opposite side of the loch from Sconser are the crofting communities known as **The Braes**, who successfully opposed their landlords' eviction notices and brought the crofters' cause to the public's attention (see box, page 35).

Isle of Raasay → *OS Landranger No 24.*

The lush and beautiful island of Raasay lies only a few miles off the east coast of Skye, yet despite its attractions it is all too often ignored by the tourist hordes. The island is a nature conservancy, where you may see seals, eagles and otters. Its hilly terrain and superb cliff scenery also offer numerous walking opportunities, the best of which is to the distinctive flat-topped summit of **Dun Caan**, the island's highest point at 1456 ft. The views from the top are amongst the finest in Scotland. Raasay falls away to the sea, with the Cuillins on one side and the peaks of Torridon and Kintail on the other, shouldering past one another, their great blunt heads bumping the clouds. The walk to the top of the extinct volcano, via an old iron mine, is relatively straightforward and one of the most rewarding anywhere in the islands. So much so, in fact, that Boswell was inspired to dance a Highland jig on reaching the top in 1773, during his grand tour with Dr Johnson. Another excellent walk starts from North Fearns, at the end of a road running east from **Inverarish**, to the deserted township of **Hallaig**, down

Gaelic spread

Outside the Outer Hebrides, Skye is the most important centre of Gaelic culture, with a large proportion of the island's population speaking Gaelic in everyday life. This in itself is remarkable given the significant drop in population during the Clearances and the continued undermining of Gaelic culture ever since, especially through the State education system.

Today, as in other parts of the Hebrides, the native culture is again under threat, this time from the huge influx of 'white settlers' from the south, but there is also a new-found pride and interest in the Gaelic language. This has been helped by the existence of the Gaelic college on Sleat, through Gaelic writers such as the late Sorley Maclean, a radical local newspaper (The West Highland Free Press), economic support from Highlands and Islands Enterprise, and spiritual under-pinning from the Sabbatarian Free Church. Gaelic is being taught again in schools and can be heard on television. The ancient heritage of the Highlands and Islands is fighting back and reasserting itself as a major European culture.

the side of Beinn na Leac and back to North Fearns. The circular route is 5 miles long.

Raasay was for much of its history the property of the Macleods of Lewis, whose chief residence was the ruined **Brochel Castle**, before moving to **Clachan**, where **Raasay House** is now located. The original Raasay House was torched by government troops after Culloden, along with all the island's houses and its boats, as punishment for the Macleods giving refuge to Bonnie Prince Charlie. After the Macleods sold the island in 1843, the Clearances began in earnest and Raasay suffered a long period of emigration, depopulation and poverty. It is not surprising, then, that the island's most famous son, the great poet **Sorley Maclean**, wrote so passionately about this lost society. Born in Oskaig in 1911, he wrote in his native Gaelic as well as in English, and is highly regarded internationally. He died in 1996. Raasay's population now numbers around 150 and the island is a bastion of the Free Church, whose strict Sabbatarian beliefs should be respected by visitors.

Those who make it to the north of the island may wish to note that the 2 miles of road linking **Brochel** to **Arnish** were the work of one man, Calum Macleod. He decided to build the road himself after the council turned down his requests for proper access to his home. He spent between 10 and 15 years building it with the aid of a pick, a shovel, a wheelbarrow and a road-making manual which cost him three shillings. He died in 1988, soon after its completion, and it continues to be known as 'Calum's Road'. For an account of Calum's Road, read the book of that name penned by the journalist and author, Roger Hutchinson.

Sleat Peninsula → For listings, see pages 40-47. Phone code 01471.

East of Broadford is the turn-off to the peninsula of Sleat (pronouned 'slate'), a part of the island so uncharacteristically green and fertile that it's known as 'The Garden of Skye'. Sleat is another entry point to the island. Ferries cross from Mallaig on the mainland to Armadale on the southeastern shore of the peninsula. While the rest of the island is the preserve of the Macleods, Sleat is MacDonald country. The MacDonalds of Sleat are one of the major surviving branches of Clan Donald, and have the right to use the title Lord MacDonald (but not Lord of the Isles, which is now used by the heir to the throne).

Isle Ornsay

South of Duisdale is the signed turning for Isle Ornsay, or Eilean Iarmain (pronounced *eelan yarman*) in Gaelic, a very beautiful place in a small rocky bay overlooking the tidal Isle of Ornsay with the mountains of Knoydart in the background. This was once Skye's main fishing port, and the neat whitewashed cottages and tiny harbour are still here. It is also largely Gaelic-speaking, thanks mainly to the efforts of its landlord, Sir Iain Noble, who owns the hotel (see Sleeping, page 46) and his own local Gaelic whisky company as well as the northern half of the peninsula, which is known as Fearan Eilean Iarmain.

A few miles further on is a turn-off to the left which leads to the villages of **Ord**, **Tokavaig** and **Tarskavaig**, on the west coast of the peninsula, from where, on a clear day, there are views across to the Cuillins. Near Tokavaig is the ruin of **Dunsgaith Castle**, home of the MacDonalds of Sleat until the 17th century. Tarskavaig is a typical crofting township. In the early 19th century the MacDonalds claimed the more fertile glens inland for their sheep farms and evicted the people to coastal townships like Tarskavaig. Just beyond the turn-off to Ord are the remains of **Knock Castle**, yet another MacDonald stronghold.

Ostaig

At Ostaig is the Gaelic College, **Sabhal Mor Ostaig** ① *T01471-888000*, founded by Sir Iain Noble. All subjects are taught in Gaelic, including full-time courses in business studies and media, as well as short courses in Gaelic music and culture during the summer months. The bookshop has a good selection of books and tapes for those wishing to learn the language. Ostaig is also the beginning or end (depending on which direction you're heading) of the detour to Tarskavaig, Tokavaig and Ord.

Armadale to the Point of Sleat

Just before the ferry pier at Armadale is **Armadale Castle** ① *T01471-844305, www. clandonald.com, Apr-Oct daily 0930-1730, £6, concessions £4, Nov-Mar shops and gardens open 1000-1600*, which was built in 1815 as the main residence of the MacDonalds of Sleat. Most of the castle is now a roofless ruin but the servants' quarters contain an excellent exhibition and accompanying video explaining the history of the Lordship of the Isles. The Clan Donald Lords of the Isles took over from their Norse predecessors in ruling the Hebrides until their power was broken in 1493. The former stables at the entrance comprise offices, a restaurant and bookshop, while the estate manager's house has been converted to accommodate an extensive library and archives. The castle is surrounded by 40 acres of handsome gardens and woodland, and there are ranger-led walks along nature trails with fine views across to the mainland.

Just beyond Armadale Castle is the tiny village of **Armadale**, which is strung out along the wooded shoreline and merges into the neighbouring village of **Ardvasar** (pronounced Ard-vaa-sar), which has a post office and general store. Armadale's raison d'être is the ferry pier and there's not a huge amount to keep you occupied except for Ragamuffin, T01471-844217, a friendly shop famed for its colourful knitwear and quirky gifts. Also on the ferry pier is the excellent **Seafari** boat trip operator (see Activities and tours, page 47). About four or five miles past the ferry port, at the end of the road, is **Aird of Sleat**, a crofting township, from where you walk out to the lighthouse at the **Point of Sleat**. It's a 5-mile walk on a clear path across moorland with fine coastal scenery.

Isle of Skye listings

For Sleeping and Eating price codes and other relevant information, see pages 12-18.

◎ Sleeping

Skye does not lack quality accommodation to suit every budget, though in the busy summer season it's strongly advised to book ahead. The local TICs have lists of available accommodation and for a small fee will book it for you. See also www.skye.co.uk.

Portree *p27, map p28*

There are several guesthouses on Bosville Terr and many B&Bs on Stormyhill Rd and the streets running off it. Prices tend to be slightly higher in Portree than the rest of the island, though B&Bs on the outskirts of town are usually cheaper. There's also an excellent campsite and two good backpackers.

££££ Cuillin Hills Hotel, off road north to Staffin, on the edge of town, T01478-612003, www.cuillinhills-hotel-skye.co.uk. Open all year. 28 rooms. Set in 15 acres of gardens overlooking the bay. Variety of rooms at different rates – ask for front rooms with views of harbour and hills . The highly regarded View restaurant is set in a gallery space, while the informal brasserie hosts jazz concerts

££££-£££ Bosville Hotel, Bosville Terr, T01478-612846, www.bosvillehotel.co.uk. 18 rooms. Comfortable and stylish accommodation in central, upmarket hotel with views across the harbour. Enjoy a malt in the Merchant Bar – once the village bank. The Chandlery Restaurant is one of the best on Skye (see Eating, page 44).

£££ Marmalade, Home Farm Rd, T01478-611711, www.marmaladehotels.com. Open all year. Recently refurbished, this Georgian period building with views across the harbour boasts seven en suite contemporary styled rooms (including family) and great value restaurant (including Sun roast) and bar food. Lovely gardens and family friendly.

£££ Viewfield House Hotel, on the road into Portree from the south, T01478-612217, www.viewfieldhouse.com. Open mid-Apr to mid-Oct. 11 bedrooms. A 200-year-old country house full of antiques, set in 20 acres of woodland garden. Good food and old-world hospitality, and the log fire adds to the welcoming atmosphere. Has a charming 5-bedroom cottage suitable for family self-catering, £450-700 per week.

££ Otterburn, Coolin Hills Estate, T01478-613588. 2 rooms. A cosy B&B with stunning views over Portree and harbour.

£ Bayfield Backpackers, T01478-612231, www.skyehostel.co.uk. Another central hostel, with 24 beds. Clean and friendly with all amenities just mins from the door.

£ Portree Independent Hostel, Old Post Office, The Green, T01478-613737. 60 beds. Right in the centre of town, 100 yds from the town square. Laundrette, Internet access in the lounge and kitchen.

Camping

There's a well maintained, friendly campsite with great showers at Torvaig, 2 miles north of Portree centre, T01478-611849, Apr-Oct.

Trotternish Peninsula *p29*

£££ Flodigarry Country House Hotel, a few miles north of Staffin, T01470-552203, www.flodigarry.co.uk. Beautifully located at the foot of the mighty Quiraing and with stunning views across Staffin Bay, this is one of the great country house hotels, with a relaxing old-world atmosphere and restaurant. Flora MacDonald's cottage is in the grounds and has been tastefully refurbished, giving the chance to stay in a place steeped in the island's history. The lively bar is a good place to enjoy a laugh and a jig.

£££ Uig Hotel, on the right of the road into Uig from Portree, beside a white church, opposite Frazer's Folly, T01470-542205, www.uighotel.com. Open all year. 16 en suite rooms. Comfortable accommodation in a traditional country house with great views across the bay, good food and a friendly island welcome.

££ Cuil Lodhe Guest House, Cuill, Uig, T01470-542216. Open all year. 3 en suite rooms. Cosy B&B set on shore of Uig Bay, all rooms with sea views.

££ Duntulm Castle Hotel, near Duntulm Castle, T01470-552213, www.duntulm castle.co.uk. Open Mar-Nov. Friendly and homely with great views across the Minch to the Outer Hebrides. Idyllic and good value. Also offer 3-night dinner and B&B fishing breaks (£375 per person).

££ Woodbine House, Woodbine House, Uig, T01470-542243, www.skyeactivities. co.uk. Open Easter-Oct. 5 rooms. Whitewashed stone cottage renowned for flexible room options (ideal for families) and a warm welcome.

£ Dun Flodigarry Backpackers Hostel, 100 yds from the bar of the **Flodigarry Country House Hotel**, T/F01470-552212, www.hostelflodigarry.co.uk. Open Mar-Oct. 40 beds. Clifftop seaviews and adequate facilities including laundry, drying room and kitchen. Camping also available.

£ SYHA Youth Hostel, 1 mile from the Uig ferry terminal, T01470-542746. Open mid-Mar to Oct. High above the port on the south side of the village. Offers spectacular views over the bay. Basic but comfortable, with a few family and private rooms. The warden can help arrange bike and canoe hire.

Camping
There's camping at Flodigarry Backpackers Hostel (above) and south of Staffin Bay, T01470-562213. Open mid-Apr to end Sep.

Waternish, Dunvegan and Duirinish *p31*
There are many places to stay in and around Dunvegan, and the TIC will arrange accommodation for you, T01470-521581.

££££ The House Over-By, Colbost, Dunvegan, T01470-511258, www. threechimneys.co.uk. A few yards away from the very wonderful **Three Chimneys** (see Eating, below), on Duirnish Peninsula and run by the same folk. Six sumptuous rooms, all with sea views.

££££-£££ Greshornish House Hotel, Edinbane, T01470-582266, www. greshornishhouse.com. Open all year. 8 rooms. Set in 10 acres of land at the end of a single-track road by the shores of the eponymous loch. If you're after peace and tranquillity then look no further. Head chef Colin Macdonald produces superb food in the dining room (**££££** including dinner), and there's also a billiard room, tennis court and croquet lawn for those clement days.

££££-£££ Skeabost Country House Hotel, Skeabost Bridge, 6 miles north of Portree on A850 to Dunvegan, T01470-532202, www. skeabostcountryhouse.com. Open all year. 14 rooms. This former Victorian hunting lodge on the shores of Loch Snizort, now part of the Oxford Hotels and Inns group, has a snooker room, guest lounges, a nine-hole golf course and salmon fishing on nearby River Snizort. Grand setting and grounds let down by décor that's a tad tired for the pricetag.

£££ Hillside House, 34 Lochbay, T01470-592263, www.bed-and-breakfast-on-skye. co.uk. 3 rooms. Traditional-looking house built in 2007 with clever eco-friendly facilities, light-filled rooms and jaw-dropping loch-side views.

£££ The Spoons, 75 Aird Bernisdale, T01470-532217, www.thespoonsonskye. com. Open all year. 3 rooms. A cosy hotel with luxury touches recently built and designed by owners who cut their cloth running the quality lodgings and kitchen of Eilean Shona House. Superb cooking and baking.

£££-££ Lyndale House, Edinbane, T01470-582329, www.lyndale.net. Quiet, delightful retreat hidden down a private drive off the A850 to Dunvegan. 300-year-old house with lovely views and sunsets from the sitting room. Nice touches, such as fresh flowers and bathrobes, and organic produce for breakfast. Also 3 fabulous, self-catering cottages from around £500 per week.

£££-££ Shorefield House, Edinbane, T/F01470-582444, www.shorefield-house.com. Open all year. 4 rooms. Superb B&B in modern home with flexible room options for families and groups, as well as separate self-catering accommodation. Much praised breakfasts served in bright conservatory room.

££ Crossal House, Glen Drynoch, T01478-640745, www.crossal.co.uk. Open all year. Two rooms. Homely B&B set in gardens and surrounding wilds of Glen Drynoch.

££ The Lodge at Edinbane, Edinbane, T01470-582217, www.the-lodge-at-edinbane.co.uk. Open all year. 6 en suite rooms. If it's old-world character you're after, this place has it in spades; there's even a ghost or 2. A 16th-century former hunting lodge by the shores of Loch Greshornish, it's also where to enjoy good value bar meals and restaurant fare over a malt or real ale.

Camping
£ Kinloch Campsite, Dunvegan, T01470-521531, www.kinloch-campsite.co.uk. Apr-Oct. Pleasant, small campsite with sea views and bakery, fuel, Wi-Fi and shop nearby.

The Cuillins and Minginish *p34*
£££ Sligachan Hotel, 7 miles south of Portree, where the A87 Kyleakin–Portree road meets the A863 to Dunvegan, T01471-865 0204 www.sligachan.co.uk. With the Cuillins almost at its back door, this is the legendary rallying point for climbers (though it also has its fair share of more sedentary guests). 21 refurbished bed- rooms, a genteel MacKenzies bar and a rather barnlike though lively **Seamus** bar, which stocks a selection of malts and also serves the island's real ales and hearty (🍴) meals. There's also a 20-bed bunkhouse (Mar-Oct) and a campsite, although there's superb and free wild camping just up river.

££ Coruisk House, on the right-hand side just after the Elgol village sign on the road from Broadford, T01471-866330, www.seafood-skye.co.uk. Open Apr-Sep. Restaurant with all rooms en suite. Worth coming here for the freshest of seafood (lunch 🍴, dinner

🍴), which can be enjoyed al fresco (they have a Midge Master). Also has a self-catering cottage and traditional crofthouse for rent.

££ Rowan Cottage, a mile east at Glasnakille, T01471-866287, www.rowancottage-skye.co.uk. Open mid-Mar to end Nov. Attractive B&B that will also organize a packed lunch and supper tray on request.

£ Croft Bunkhouse, Wigwams & Bothies, north of Carbost, near Portnalong, T01471-640254, www.skyehostels.com. Open all year. Sleeps 40 and there's also room for camping. Transport from Sligachan or Portree, rents mountain bikes, there's a pub and shop nearby.

£ Skyewalker Independent Hostel, beyond Portnalong on the road to Fiscavaig, T01471-640250, www.isleofskye-hostel.com. Now under new management, this pleasant hostel is in a converted school. Basic and clean 36 bunk accommodation with adjoining lounge area. On site café and shop, live folk music and a giant al fresco chessboard.

Camping
The well run campsite opposite **Sligachan Hotel** is possibly the most popular budget place to stay in the area, clean, central and with hot showers. There's also a campsite by the shore in Glen Brittle, T01471-640404.

Broadford and the east coast *p36*
£££-££ White Heather Hotel, Kyleakin, T01599-534577, www.whiteheatherhotel.co.uk. Open Mar-Oct. 9 en suite rooms. Friendly and welcoming small hotel overooking the harbour. Hosts, Gilllian and Craig, are very helpful and breakfasts are excellent, with views of the harbour thrown in for good measure.

££ Luib House, Luib, by Broadford, T01471-820334, www.luibhouse.co.uk. Open all year. Welcoming, rustic B&B with views over Loch Ainort. Great breakfast and will accept dogs.

££-£ Tir Alainn, 8 Upper Breakish, T01471-822366. Open all year. 3 rooms, 2 en suite. Just outside Broadford on road to Kyleakin. Pam and Ron are extremely welcoming and run a cosy B&B, offering exceptional food, good views, comfy guest lounge and expert mountain-guide advice.

£ Dun Caan Hostel, near the old ferry quay, Kyleakin, T01599-534087, www.skyerover. co.uk. Open all year. Of all the hostels around this part of the island, this one stands out for the personal service. Clean and cosy and packed with information on the local area and Skye. Bike hire available. Recommended.

£ Skye Backpackers Hostel, Kyleakin, T01599-534510, www.scotlandstophostels. com. Another budget option with the pub and ruin of Castle Maol close at hand.

Self-catering

Fossil Cottage, a mile or so south of Broadford, at Lower Breakish off the A87 to Kyleakin, T01471-822297, www.fossil-cottage-skye.co.uk. Has been beautifully converted from a 15-year-old croft (and recently a bothy) to a 1-bedroom, TV-free zone right by the water. From £320-£560 per week.

Isle of Raasay *p37*

££ Borodale House (the original name of the house in 1870), on the Isle of Raasay near to the Outdoor Centre, T/F01478-660222, www.isleofraasayhotel.co.uk. Open all year. Extensively refurbished and formerly known as the Isle of Raasay Hotel, with 12 en suite rooms, a lovely **Cuillin View Restaurant** (ⓘ-ⓘ) serving tasty lunches and dinners that include locally reared venison. Sea views.

£ Raasay Outdoor Centre, T01478-660266, www.raasayoutdoorcentre.co.uk. The main settlement on the island is Inverarish, a 15-min walk from the ferry dock. Half a mile further is this centre housed in the huge, 259 year-old Georgian mansion that was Raasay House. Offers basic accommodation for backpackers, families and educational groups. After a day's exertions on sea and land, refuel with the home-baking, hearty fare and real ales served by the good value **Dolphin café/restaurant** (0900-2300, evening meals 1830-2100).

£ SYHA Hostel, Creachan Cottage, T01478-660240. Open mid-Mar to end-Oct. Reached via a rough track leading up a steep hill from tiny Oskaig. Basic, rustic 20-bed hostel. 2-mile walk to the nearest shop.

Sleat Peninsula *p38*

££££ Hotel Eilean Iarmain, Isle Ornsay, T01471-833332, www.eilean-iarmain.co.uk. 12 rooms. Award-winning Victorian hotel full of charm and old-world character, with wonderful views. It is lovely and romantic, and an absolute must if you're in the area and can afford it. Its award-winning restaurant features local shellfish landed only yds away (open to non-residents). A cheaper option is to eat in the cosy bar next door, which serves pub grub of an impossibly high standard in a more informal atmosphere. The hotel also offers winter shooting on the local estate, and you can enjoy a tasting of the local whisky.

££££ Kinloch Lodge, at the head of Loch na Dal, T01471-833333, www.claire-macdonald. com. The track that leads to the 19th-century **Sporting Lodge** turns off the A851 about eight miles south of Broadford. Lord and Lady MacDonald's family home oozes comfort and refined style with its antiques, prints and classy touches such as Egyptian cotton sheets. This is also a place to enjoy one of Scotland's finest culinary experiences in the grandest of settings. Lady Claire MacDonald is one of the best-known cooks in Scotland and author of several cookbooks, and if you do decide to treat yourself make sure you leave enough room for their exquisite puddings. The 5-course fixed menu is in our expensive range, but well worth it.

££££-£££ Duisdale Hotel, Duisdale, T01471-833202, www.duisdale.com. Extensively refurbished, this former Hunting Lodge which boasts 17 individually styled rooms (2 with 4-poster beds), tasty lunch, afternoon tea, and dinner fare that draws on the local seafood. Has a fabulous Chart Room in which to savour a malt. There's also the chance to enjoy a day's sail of the offshore islands aboard its private 42-ft yacht.

££££-£££ Toravaig House Hotel, Knock Bay, Teangue, T01471-820200, www.skye

hotel.co.uk. Open all year. 9 plush and contemporary en suite rooms. This was voted Scottish Island Hotel of the Year in 2005 and 2007, and its Islay Restaurant won Highlands and Islands Restaurant of the Year 2009-2010. Perfect for those seeking peace and quiet and a romantic break. It's isolated for those who like a pub within walking distance, but why go elsewhere when you're surrounded by such luxury.

£££ Ardvasar Hotel, in Ardvasar, near ferry terminal, T01471-844223, www.ardvasar hotel.com. Traditional whitewashed coaching inn with 9 rooms, an excellent restaurant and the liveliest pub in the vicinity.

£ Flora MacDonald Hostel, Kilmore, between the turning for Isle Ornsay and Armadale, T01471-844440, www.isle-of-skye-tour-guide. co.uk. Clean and friendly 20-bed hostel, offering free transport to and from Armadale Pier.

Eating

There are notable exceptions, including the magnificent **Three Chimneys** restaurant, but some of the best food on Skye is to be found in hotel dining rooms, so also check the Sleeping section for places to eat. Many B&Bs also provide evening meals on request.

Portree p27, map p28

Chandlery Seafood Restaurant, Bosville Hotel, see Sleeping. Run by chef John Kelly, who trained at the Savoy, this restaurant serves exquisite fine food, drawing on the local larder of fresh meats and fish. Oozes style and ambience. The best in town.

Café Arriba, Quay Brae, T01478-611830. Daily 0700-1700, 1800-late. A cosy, bright place with a slightly bohemian air, serving mouth-watering breakfasts, lunches and dinners to suit vegetarians and meat-eaters alike. A starter can include the eastern Dukkah aromatic spice mix or try a main of venison and apricot, or butterbean and apricot korma.

Harbour View Seafood Restaurant, 7 Bosville Terr, T01478-612069. Apr-Oct

1200-2200. Freshest of seafood in cosy surroundings. Good 2nd choice after **Chandlery** and offering a good selection of fine wines to accompany mouth-watering daily specials.

Sea Breezes Restaurant, right by the pier, T01478-612016. Open daily. This snug, bright restaurant will delight the seafood lover and steak afficionado alike. It's not the cheapest in town but you're assured of quality and ambience. Early bird, 2 course dinner from 1700-1800 (£18). Recommended.

The Chip Shop on the pier and directly next door to the busy **Lower Deck Seafood Restaurant**. Open until 2100 daily. A great option for simple, no frills fast food, with guaranteed fresh fish. On the author's visit it ran out of fish and chips. Now that's popular!

Trotternish Peninsula p29

Pieces of Ate, in the village of Staffin, T01470-562787. Tue-Thu 1030-1630, Fri-Sat 1030-2030, Sun 1100-1500. A great place for home-made soups, bacon rolls, sandwiches, coffee, home-bakes and deli produce.

Pub an the Pier, Uig. Open until 2300. Cheap bar meals, and the famous Cuillin ales are brewed at the nearby Skye Brewery. You can also change foreign currency here.

Waternish, Dunvegan and Duirinish p31

The Three Chimneys, Duirnish Peninsula, Calbost, T01470-511258, www. threechimneys. co.uk. Mon-Sat 1230-1400, 1830-2130. Savour the creative dishes produced by head chef Michael Smith and his team and you'll appreciate why this remote dining experience is considered one of the best in the country. Indeed, some guests even fly to Skye just to experience it. Also accommodation (**££££**).

Lochbay Seafood, Waternish Peninsula, T01470-592235, www.lochbay-seafood-restaurant.co.uk. Open Apr-Oct Sun-Fri for lunch and until 2100. You should finish off the day with a meal at this wonderful restaurant where you can almost see your dinner being landed. Book ahead.

††††-†† Stein Inn, Waternish, T01470-592362, www.steininn.co.uk. Bar meals Mon-Sat 1200-1600, 1800-2130, Sun 1230-1600, 1800-2100. Reputedly the oldest inn on Skye, book a table here and enjoy a real ale or malt before feasting on venison or shellfish. If you over indulge, there's accommodation (**££**).

Broadford and the east coast *p36*
†††-†† Creelers Restaurant, just off main road behind the Serpentarium, T01471-822281. Open Tue-Sat (also some Mon's), 1200-1000. Bright, sea-facing restaurant adorned with artwork. Attentive, friendly staff serve simple, appetizing seafood, memorable desserts and a tapas option, Recommended.
†† Red Skye Restaurant, Breakish, T01471 822180 www.redskyerestaurant.co.uk. Open Mon-Sun, 1200-2100 (last orders). Housed in the handsome old village schoolhouse, this newish addition to the Skye dining scene is proving popular with punters from near and far. Head chef Campbell MacFadyen's creative take on traditional and Mediterranean dishes complements the modern décor and relaxed atmosphere. Expect hearty Scots favourites like Cullen skink and Skye haggis alongside juicy salads.
††-† Claymore Bar-Restaurant, south end of Broadford, T01471-822333. Decent bar meals.
Kinloch Lodge, Sleat, T01471-833333. Open daily in high season. Lady Claire Macdonald's renowned restaurant may be pricey but head chef Marcello Tully's inventive, changing menus (from £52 per person) based on seasonal and local produce are perfect for that special dining occasion in the Garden of Skye. Reservations essential.

🍷 Bars and pubs

Portree *p27, map p28*
The town's nightlife is mainly confined to eating and drinking. The **Pier Hotel**, Quay St, T01478-612094, by the harbour, is a real fishermen's drinking den; the refurbished **Royal Hotel**, Bank St, T01478-612525, is also popular; for reasonable bar food (**††**) until

1000, and a younger crowd, head just past the square to the **Isles Inn** at the end of Wentworth St.

Waternish, Dunvegan and Duirinish *p31*
Stein Inn, see Eating and Sleeping above. There are few pleasures in life equal to sitting outside this venerable old pub with a pint of ale from the local Isle of Skye brewery and tucking into an excellent pub supper (**†††-††**) while watching a Hebridean sunset. On less clement evenings the old peat-burning fire inside provides an alternative feel-good factor.

🎭 Entertainment

Portree *p27, map p28*
Aros Experience, see page 28. Call the box office for details of their monthly programme, T01478-613750. Has a theatre which shows drama, movies and live music.
Portree Community Centre, Camanahd Sq, Park Rd, T01478-613736. The place to come if you fancy a wild Fri night ceilidh though pubs like the **Isles Inn** by the town square also hold occasional live music/ceilidh nights.

🎪 Festivals and events

Portree *p27, map p28*
Early Aug Highland Games, www.skye-highland-games.co.uk, tickets £8, children £4. A one-day event held in Portree. These games, first held in 1877, include traditional highland dancing and piping competitions.

🛍 Shopping

Portree *p27, map p28*
There's a **Co-op** supermarket, diagonally opposite the Bosville Hotel, and a large **Tesco** supermarket on the road to Uig.
Carbostcraft Pottery, Bayfield Rd. Pottery in a variety of designs. Also have a shop near the Talisker Distillery, see page 35.
Crocks & Rocks, Main St. Hebridean jewellery.
Over the Rainbow, at the top of Quay Brae, T01478-612555. Open 0900-2200 in the

high season. A good place to buy woollens.
Skye Batiks, the Green, near the TIC, T01478-613331. Sells handmade 'batiks' (colourful cotton fabrics), which are pricey but unique souvenirs from Skye, see also page 32.
Skye Woollen Mill, Dunvegan Rd, T01478-612889. Knitwear and tartan souvenirs.

The Cuillins and Minginish *p34*
Cioch Direct, 4 Ullinish, Struan, T01470-572307. For mountain gear.
Ragamuffin, T01470 844217, at Armadale's ferry pier in Sleat. Filled with vibrant knitwear and interesting gifts.
Skyeskyns, 17 Lochbay, Waternish, T01470-592237. A fascinating place to learn about a traditional tannery and peruse pelts turned into fabulous rugs and throws.

⚙ Activities and tours

Portree *p27, map p28*
If the weather's good, Portree offers a wide variety of outdoor activities.

Boat trips
MV Stardust boat trips, Portree Harbour, T07798-743858, www.skyeboat-trips.co.uk. Sail daily from the pier, and offer a range of cruises, fishing forays and wildlife trips (£12-25), including the chance to spot the rare white-tailed sea eagle, as well as to see the seals at Griana Sgeir and the birdlife at Holm Island. Trips can also be made to Rona, north of Raasay, £18 per person, children £9.

Trotternish Peninsula *p29*
Whitewave Activities, a few miles north of Uig, on the A855 at Linicrowhere, T01471-542414, www.white-wave.co.uk. Here you can try windsurfing, rock climbing, archery, walking and sea kayaking. There's also a café specializing in vegetarian, seafood and Celtic music, and a B&B.

Uig *p29*
Skye Activities, Woodbine Guest House, Uig, T01470-542243. Boat trips on a nippy 6-m

rib, wildlife watching, fishing and charters. Mountain biking, archery and waterskiing too.

The Cuillins and Minginish *p34*
Boat trips
Bella Jane Boat Trips, Elgol, T0800-731 3089, www.bellajane.co.uk. Trips to Rùm or Canna. From £12.50 for a 1½-hr trip.
Fast-Boat, T0845-224 2219, www.fast-boat. net. Private charter along Skye's coastline, Raasay, the Small Isles and even to Harris. From £280 per day including skipper and boat.
Misty Isle Boat Trips, Sealladh na Mara, Elgol, T01471-866288, www.mistyisleboat trips. co.uk. Makes the spectacular trip from Elgol into the gaping maw of Loch Coruisk, One of the highlights of any trip to Skye. 3 hrs, including 1½ hrs ashore, £18, children £7.50. You should be able to see seals and porpoises en route. There's also a one-way trip for experienced walkers/climbers (£12.50 adult, children £7.50) who wish to make the return journey on foot or to explore the Cuillins.

Climbing
Some of the guides who offer climbing on Skye are: **Guiding on Skye**, George Yeomans, T01478-650380, www.guidingonskye.co.uk, also offers bushcraft and survival instruction; **Richard MacGuire**, 4 Matheson Pl, Portree, T01478-613180, www.blavenguiding.co.uk, operating since 1995; **Skye Guides**, Mike Lates, 3 Luib, Broadford, T01471-822116, www.skyeguides.co.uk.

Fishing
Skye Ghillie Fly Fishing, 4 Windsor Cres, Portree, T01478-611533, www.skyeghilliefly fishing.co.uk. Salmon and sea-trout fishing, guiding, and ghillie services and tuition.

Isle of Raasay *p37*
Raasay Outdoor Centre, see Sleeping, above, T01478-660266, www.raasayoutdoor centre.co.uk. This reputable operator runs various adventure courses, from climbing to sailing. Also offers basic accommodation.

Sleat Peninsula *p38*
Seafari, T01471-833316, T01471-844787, www.seafari.co.uk. 1- and 2-hr wildlife trips 3-hr whale-spotting trips and a day trip from the pier at Armadale. £15-£100.

⊖ Transport

Portree *p27, map p28*
Bus There are buses (No 57A) Mar-Oct Mon-Sat around the Trotternish Peninsula, in each direction, via **Uig**. Daily buses to **Kyleakin**, and to **Armadale** via **Broadford**. There are buses Mon-Sat to **Carbost** (for the Talisker Distillery). Also use this service to access **Glenbrittle**, alighting at Carbost and walking eight miles. There are buses daily Mon-Sat to **Glendale** via **Dunvegan**, and buses Mon-Sat to **Waternish** via **Dunvegan**.
Cycle hire Island Cycles, the Green, T01478-613121. Mon-Sat 1000-1700, hire mountain bikes. Isle of Skye Trekking and Riding Centre, near Suladale and about 10 miles west of Portree towards Dunvegan, T01470-582419, www.theisleofskyetrekkingcentre. co.uk, friendly and fully trained staff. Trekking and horse riding for all ages and abilities.
Taxis A2B Taxis, T01478-613456; Ace Taxis, T01478-613600.

Trotternish Peninsula *p29*
Bus Scottish Citylink runs a service to **Inverness**, **Fort William** and **Glasgow**. For more information, see Ins and outs, page 27.
Ferry From **Uig** to **Lochmaddy** on **North Uist** (1 hr 45 mins) and to **Tarbert** on **Harris** (1 hr 45 mins). For details see page 26, or contact Uig, T01470-542219.

The Cuillins and Minginish *p34*
Bus To **Portree** via **Sligachan** from **Portnalong**, take the No 53 bus that runs Mon-Sat. The same service stops at the Talisker Distillery, Carbost.

If you've walked into the remote areas of Glenbrittle and Eynort, the only option is to walk out for 8 miles until you meet the B8009, where you can pick-up the No 53 at

Carbost to return to Drynoch junction on the A863. Here you can either stay on the No 53 to **Sligachan** and **Portree**, or wait for the No 56B **Portree** to **Dunvegan** service that stops (schooldays only) at **Drynoch** and heads north to **Struan** and Dunvegan Hotel.

Broadford and the east coast *p36*
Bus Daily Citylink buses run from **Broadford** to **Portree**, **Inverness** and **Fort William**. Buses run daily to **Kyleakin**, **Portree** and **Armadale/Ardvasar**. There are buses from **Kyleakin** to **Portree** via **Broadford**, to **Armadale** and **Ardvasar** via Broadford (Mon-Sat) and every 30 mins to **Kyle of Lochalsh**, see page 252, via the Skye Bridge.
Car hire S Morrison Ltd Broom Pl, Portree T01478-612688, www.portreecoachworks. co.uk. From around £40 per day.
Cycle hire Fairwinds Bicycle Hire, 4th house on left past Broadford Hotel, T01471-822270. Mar-Oct. Rents bikes from £10 per day.
Ferry CalMac car and passenger ferry from **Sconser** to **Raasay** several times daily Mon-Sat, twice on Sun, 25 mins, £5.65 per passenger return, £22 per car, bicycles free.

Sleat Peninsula *p38*
No 52/55 Bus Mon-Sat from **Ardvasar and nearby Armadale Pier** to **Portree** (1 hr 20 mins) and **Kyleakin** (1 hr) via **Broadford** (40 mins). 1st bus leaves at 0940.
Ferry For crossings to Mallaig, see page 27.

ⓘ Directory

Portree *p27, map p28*
Banks Clydesdale Bank, Bank of Scotland, Somerled Sq; Royal Bank of Scotland, Bank St. **Internet** Portree Backpacker's Hostel, Dunvegan Rd; Portree Independent Hostel, see Sleeping page 40; the TIC. **Laundry** Portree Independent Hostel, see Sleeping, page40. **Post** Post office, top of Quay Brae.

Broadford and the east coast *p36*
Banks Bank of Scotland, by the shops opposite the road to the new pier, Broadford.

The Small Isles

These four tenacious little siblings are a world away from the Scottish mainland and not for the faint or fickle traveller. It almost takes longer to reach them from London than it does to fly to Australia, so you have to be pretty determined. Those who do make it this far are rewarded with perfect peace and an almost primeval silence and solitude. This is nature in the glorious, unabashed raw; a slow-moving, sepia-tinged counterpoint to the frenetic pace and special effects of 21st-century life. ⟩⟩ *For listings, see pages 52-54.*

Ins and outs

Getting there

A CalMac passenger-only ferry sails from Mallaig to at least two of the islands once daily. Saturday is your only opportunity to step ashore on all four of the islands. For the latest seasonal timetable visit www.calmac.co.uk

From April to September the CalMac ferries from Mallaig are supplemented by cruises from Arisaig with **Arisaig Marine** ① *T01687-450224, www.airsaig.co.uk*, aboard *MV Shearwater*. There's a good chance of seeing dolphins, seals, porpoises and even whales during the bumpy ride. ⟩⟩ *For further details, see page 243, and Transport page 53.*

Eigg

→ *For listings, see pages 52-54. Phone code 01687.*
Little Eigg (pronounced *egg*), only 5 miles long by 3 miles wide, has had something of a chequered past. In 1577 it was the scene of one of the bloodiest episodes in the history of clan warfare (see box, page 30). More recently it has been at the heart of a bitter land ownership debate. Having en- dured a succession of absentee landlords, ranging from the merely eccentric to the criminally negligent, the 70 remaining islanders seized the moment in 1997 and bought the island themselves, in conjunction with the Scottish Wildlife Trust. In February 2008, Eigg's own solar, wind and hydro- powered electricity supply was switched on. The island's wildlife includes

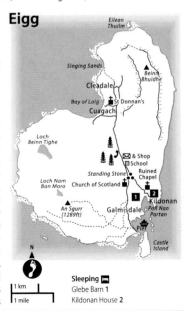

Eigg

Sleeping 🛏
Glebe Barn 1
Kildonan House 2

The end of an era

George Bullough and his wife, Lady Monica, brought a slice of Belgravia to the tiny Hebridean island of Rùm. Every autumn the family showed up to stalk deer and throw lavish parties for the glitterati and aristocracy of the day. Guests would be met at the pier by chauffeur-driven Albion cars while those arriving by ferry would step into a horse-drawn carriage, or be given a piggy-back by the castle staff when the tide was out. The outrageously wealthy Bulloughs guarded their privacy with a level of ruthlessness that would make even today's pop and film stars blush. Guns were routinely fired at passing boats to warn off any unwanted commoners and discourage the curious.

All this frivolous excess ended suddenly with the outbreak of war in 1914. George Bullough was appointed to a military post, the island's able-bodied staff were sent to the trenches to die for their country and the family's 220-ft steam-yacht, Rhouma, became a minesweeper. After the war, the Bulloughs visited less and less often and the castle began to show signs of neglect. Even the poor hummingbirds died when the heating failed. Sir George himself died in 1939 and Lady Monica abandoned the place in 1954 – literally – leaving musical instruments on the stands in the ballroom and wine in the cellar. In 1957 the Bullough family sold Rùm to the Nature Conservancy for £23,000.

otters, seals, eagles and many other birds, such as the Manx shearwater, guillemots and black- throated divers. It's worth tagging along on one of the regular walks organized by the Scottish Wildlife Trust warden, John Chester.

The island is dominated by **An Sgurr**, a distinctive 1289-ft flat-topped basalt peak with three vertical sides. It can be climbed fairly easily by its western ridge, though the last few hundred feet are precipitous, and there are superb views of the Inner Hebrides and mountains of Knoydart from the summit. Sitting in the shadow of the Sgurr, at the southeastern corner, is the main settlement, **Galmisdale**. This is where the ferries drop anchor (passengers are transferred to a smaller boat), and there's a post office, shop, craft shop, tea room and bike hire all by the pier. At the northern end is the small township of **Cleadale**, on the Bay of Laig. Just to the north are the '**Singing Sands**', a beach that makes a strange sound as you walk across it. At the end of the island's only road you'll find its most famous property, **Howlin' House**, which apparently once belonged to JRR Tolkien. More details on the island are available at www.isleofeigg.org.

Muck → For listings, see pages 52-54. Phone code 01687.

Tiny Muck, just 2 miles long by one mile wide, is the smallest of the four islands and is flat and fertile, with a beautiful shell beach. It has been owned by the MacEwan family since 1879. The island gets its unfortunate name (*muc* is Gaelic for pig) from the porpoises, or 'sea pigs', that swim round its shores. The ferry berths at **Port Mór** close to which there's a range of accommodation, including a bunkhouse and hotel. There's also a tea room and craftshop. The 38 islanders use wind power to generate their own electricity. Visit the island's website, www.islemuck.com, or www.isleofmuck.com, for more information.

Rùm → *For listings, see pages 52-54. Phone code 01687.*

Diamond-shaped Rùm, known as the Forbidden Island, is the largest of the group and the most wild, beautiful and mountainous. The island is owned and run by Scottish Natural Heritage as an enormous outdoor laboratory and research station, and most of the 30 or so inhabitants are employed by them. Studies of the red deer population are among the most important areas of their work, and access to parts of the island is restricted. This is not prohibitive, though, and there are many marked nature trails, walks and birdwatching spots. The island is a haven for wildlife and perhaps its most notable resident is the magnificent white-tailed sea eagle, successfully re-introduced on to Rùm in the 1980s and now spreading beyond the island. Rùm is also home to golden eagles, Manx shearwaters and, less appealingly, millions of midges. The island is the wettest of the Small Isles and a haven for the little buggers.

Ins and outs

Ferries are anchored at the new pier, at the mouth of Loch Scresort, from where it's a 15-minute walk to Kinloch Castle. The castle stands at the head of narrow Loch Scresort by the little hamlet of **Kinloch**, where you'll find the one-and-only shop, and the community hall which also operates a tea room.

Rùm

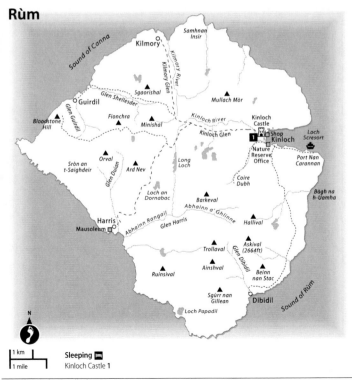

1 km
1 mile

Sleeping 🛏
Kinloch Castle 1

Kinloch Castle

ⓘ *By daily guided tour only (1 hr), and timed to coincide with the arrival of the ferry, £7 children £3.50, ask at the hostel for details.*

Though it looks like a wilderness, Rùm once supported a population of 300. Most of them were shipped off to Canada in the mid-19th century, leaving behind an uninhabited deer forest for sporting millionaires. One of these, John Bullough, a cotton millionaire from Accrington, bought it in 1888 and passed it on to his son, Sir George Bullough, who built the extravagant and extraordinary Kinloch Castle. No expense was spared on this massive late-Victorian mansion, built in 1900 at a cost of £250,000 (which equates to £15 million today). It took 300 men nearly three years to build Bullough's dream, using red Annan sandstone from Dumfrieshire shipped by puffer from the mainland. For the gardens, 250,000 tons of soil were shipped from Ayrshire and used for planting exotic specimens collected from around the world. A nine-hole golf course and bowling green were laid out, along with a Japanese-style garden and huge walled garden. Hothouses were built to grow tropical fruits, and palm houses were home to hummingbirds, turtles and even alligators. One of these creatures escaped, only to be shot by Bullough to prevent them 'interfering with the comfort of the guests'. As well as the elaborate carvings, wood panelling, furniture and flooring, the castle also incorporated many state-of-the-art features such as an electricity generator, central heating, air conditioning and an internal telephone system (the first private residence in Scotland to do so). Pride of place, however, went to the magnificent Orchestrion, a fantastical mechanical contraption that simulated a 40-piece orchestra and belted out military marches, polkas, operatic excerpts and popular tunes of the day from its position under the main staircase. It is still in working order and visitors today will be treated to a surreal rendition of *The Liberty Bell March* (the Monty Python theme tune to you and me).

In 2003 Kinloch Castle was a finalist in the BBC's first *Restoration* series, though plans to continue its costly restoration have reportedly currently stalled. Note that visitors must take off their shoes as they are escorted round the lavish rooms, many of them fading, peeling or leaking. The castle is testament to Edwardian wealth and extravagance and the tour is worth the boat trip alone. You can even stay at the castle; in the hostel which occupies the former servants' quarters.

Island walks

Rùm's other great attraction is its mountain range, which offers some of the best island mountain treks outside the Cuillins of Skye. The highest point is **Askival** (2664 ft), which can be reached by the main ridge from **Halliva**, though the route involves some rock scrambling and is only advised for fit and experienced walkers. Before setting out, ask permission from the reserve office at the **White House** ⓘ *T01687-462026, Mon-Fri 0900-1230*.

The Bullough family mausoleum, built in the style of a Greek Doric temple, stands incongruously on the west coast at **Harris Bay**. It's an interesting seven and a half mile walk across to the mausoleum from Kinloch. A less strenuous alternative is the **Kinloch Glen Trail**, which is signposted by the stone bridge as you head from the castle to the farmstead. The circular route is two and a half miles and takes a leisurely one to two hours.

Canna → *For listings, see pages 52-54.*

Canna is the most westerly of the Small Isles and is owned by the National Trust for Scotland (NTS). It's a small island, five miles long by one mile wide, bounded by cliffs and with a rugged interior, fringed by fertile patches. It's attached to its smaller neighbour, **Sanday**, by a narrow isthmus which is covered, except at low tide. There's now also a bridge linking them. The main attraction for visitors is some fine walking. It's about a mile from the ferry jetty up to the top of **Compass Hill** (458 ft), so called because its high metallic content distorts compasses. The highest point on the island is **Carn a' Ghaill** (690 ft). During the summer, a day trip from Mallaig allows you over nine hours in which to explore Canna and enjoy the fantastic views across to Rùm and Skye.

The population of 20 mostly work on the island's farm. Canna was gifted to the National Trust by its benevolent owner, the late Dr John Lorne Campbell, a notable Gaelic scholar. The island continues to be run as a single working farm and, since it was sold in 1938, has been an unofficial bird sanctuary with 157 recorded bird species, including Manx shearwater and puffins. In 2008, after a £500,000, two-year eradication project to protect the seabird population, the NTS officially declared the entire island rat-free.

The Small Isles listings

For Sleeping and Eating price codes and other relevant information, see pages 12-18.

● Sleeping

Eigg *p48, map p48*
In addition to the options below, self-catering cottages and camping are also available. For details, visit www.isleofeigg.org.
£££ Lageorna, T01687-482405, www. lageorna.com. Green Tourism Scheme B&B offering 2 rooms, self catering options and excellent food in its restaurant (£20 for 4 courses).
£ The Glebe Barn, T01687-482417, www.glebebarn.co.uk. Open Apr-Oct

(all year for groups). An independent hostel and outdoor centre. Comfortable accommodation in twin, family and bunk rooms. Residential courses and retreats, self-catering or fully catered options for groups. There's a self-contained 2-person apartment (from £230 per week or £45 per night). Groceries can be pre-ordered from the local shop (T01687-482432) and delivered.

Muck *p49*
££ Port Mór House Hotel, T01678-462365. The price includes a 3-course dinner, which is also available to non-residents if they book before 1600. The restaurant specializes in seafood and all the food is home-cooked,

Canna & Sanday

Map of Canna & Sanday showing Sea of the Hebrides, Rubha Langanais, Iorcall, An t-Each, Camus Thairbearnis, Canna, Carn a' Ghaill (690ft), Beinn Tighe (585ft), Compass Hill (458ft), A'Chill Chapel, Canna House (Private), Garrisdale Point, Tarbert, Rubha Chairinis, Pier, Garrisdale, Sliabh Meadhonach (484ft), Tarbert Bay, St Edward's (disused), Dùn Channa, Srôn Ruail (419ft), Ha'aslum, School, Lighthouse Ceann an Eilein, Tallabric (192ft), Sanday, An Stèidh, N, 1 km, 1 mile, Sound of Canna, Dùn Mòr with the lamb sourced from a local farm and the venison shot on the estate. Open log fires and views across to the Ardnamurchan Peninsula. You can ask permission at the tea room if you want to camp.

£ Carn Dearg, Port Mór, T01687-462371. Offers comfortable (2-bedroom) B&B accommodation with an evening meal available for £12.50 per person.

£ Godag House, between Port Mór and Gallanach, T01678-462371. Comfortable B&B, dinner is £10 extra. Family friendly.

Rùm *p50, map p50*
£ Kinloch Castle, T01687-462037. Open all year. 55-bed hostel in the old servants' quarters, with twin (£45), 4-bed and 6-bed dorms (£18) (**£**) with breakfast an additional £7.50, packed lunch £7 and 3-course dinner in the bistro at the rear of the castle, £18.50. Guests can also choose to sleep in greater privacy and comfort on a B&B basis in the castle's Oak Rooms (£55) (**£**). There's a small bar in the castle selling real ale (daily 1700-2300).

Camping
There are 2 bothies (**£**) on Rùm (Dibidal and Guirdal), run by the Mountain Bothy Association. Wild camping is also permitted (no fires) near the pier where a stand pipe provides water. You must inform the reserve manager at the **White House** if camping, T01687-462026.

Canna *p51*
Those wishing to stay can camp rough, with permission from the **NTS**, www.nts.org.uk.

Eating

The few places to stay on the islands serve food, and there's a tea room and a shop on Muck.

Eigg *p48, map p48*
There's a tea room, and a well-stocked shop at the jetty, T01687-482432, open Mon-Sat.

Rùm *p50, map p50*
The café/tea room on is housed in the village hall (always open as an escape from the rain or midges), and serves hot drinks, cakes, soup and other home-made food. It's open several afternoons a week during summer. There's also the bistro and bar at **Kinloch Castle**.

The shop has limited opening hours, depending on the islanders requirements, but is always open after 1700. Call the Reserve Office, T01687-462026, to check in advance.

Canna *p51*
There a small tea room but no shop, so you'll need to bring your own supplies.

Activities and tours

The Small Isles *p48*
The islands are rich in wildlife, with plenty of opportunities to spot seals and possibly basking sharks, porpoise and even orca whilst inter-island hopping aboard the *MV Sheerwater*, see Ins and outs, page 48.

Rùm *p50, map p50*
Visit the old boat shed by the pier, where there's a (very) small exhibition of wildlife and marine life, a reminder that Rùm is a National Nature Reserve with its colony of Manx shearwater, golden- and white-tailed sea eagles and red deer.

Transport

The Small Isles *p48*
On Eigg Muck and Rùm, walking is the primary means of transport, but you should also be able to hire a bike from the locals.
Ferry On a Mon and Thu from late Mar-late Oct, the ferry departs **Mallaig** at 1015 to arrive at **Eigg** at 1130. The Mon sailing continues to **Rùm** (1245) and **Canna** (1355), before returning to Mallaig (1750) via **Rùm** and **Eigg**. The Thu morning boat leaves **Eigg** to reach **Muck** at 1220, returns to **Eigg** for 1310 and disembarks at Mallaig at 1435.

On a Tue and Fri morning, the boat sails for **Muck** and **Eigg**, whilst the Fri afternoon sailing calls in at **Rùm** and **Canna** only. On a Wed, the boat from Mallaig calls in at **Rùm** (1135), **Canna** (1245) and **Rùm** again (1555) before returning to **Mallaig** at 1725. For more details of latest seasonal timetable, contact the **CalMac** office in Mallaig, T01687-462403. The **Fort William** train is time-tabled to await the Small Isles boats.

An adult return from **Mallaig** to **Eigg** (1 hr 15 mins direct) is £11.35; **Muck** (1 hr 40 mins direct) £17.25; **Rùm** (1 hr 20 mins direct) £16.75; **Canna** (2 hrs 15 mins via Rùm) £21.05. A non-landing cruise ticket that visits all of the islands costs £16. Bicycles now go free. .

Arisaig Marine, T01687-450224, www.arisaig.co.uk, sails daily (1100) Apr-Sep from Arisaig to **Eigg** (£18 return), Muck (£19 return) and **Rùm** (£24 return). Refer to their website for a comprehensive sailings timetable.

Eigg *p48, map p48*
Bus/taxi Davie Robertson, T01687-482494.
Cycle hire Eigg Bikes, close to An Laimhrig at the pier, call Euan Kirk, T01687-482432 (day), T01687-482405 (evening). Hires bikes from £15 per day.
Ferry For ferry information, see above.

Contents

Footprint features

Outer Hebrides

Ins and outs

Getting there

Air Flybe/Loganair fly from Glasgow to Stornoway on Lewis, Barra and Benbecula on North Uist. There are also flights from Edinburgh to Stornoway, Inverness to Stornoway, and from Benbecula to Barra and Stornoway. Eastern Airways fly from Aberdeen to Stornoway (T08703-669100, www.easternairways.com). Weather conditions are so changeable that flights are prone to delay and can be very bumpy. Flights to Barra have an added complication: they land on the beach meaning that the runway disappears twice a day under the incoming tide.

Bus For details of bus connections on Skye and on the mainland, contact **Scottish Citylink** ① *T08712-663 3334.* ▸▸ *For further details, see Transport pages 71, 80 and 94.*

Ferry CalMac car and passenger ferries sail to Stornoway (Lewis), Tarbert (Harris), Lochmaddy (North Uist), Lochboisdale (South Uist), Eriskay and Castlebay (Barra). Ferry details are given under each destination, but note that times change according to the day of the week and time of the year. For full details of ferry timetables contact **CalMac** ① *T08705-650000, www.calmac.co.uk. A 'CalMac Status' App can be downloaded free of charge from itunes. Alternatively, look on the website to see how to receive updates by text (but remember a signal is not always possible in some parts of the Islands).* Some routes, including the Stornoway to Ullapool crossing are very busy and if travelling with a car it's strongly advised to book your ticket in advance. A cost-effective and super-flexible way to get around the islands with a car is to purchase a **CalMac Island Rover** ticket. Available for eight and 15 consecutive days of travel respectively, these allow the ticket holder to travel on as many routes as you like without paying any additional fares. An eight-day passenger-only Rover ticket costs £48.50 a 15 day costs £70. An eight-day car ticket is £232, a 15 day is £348. Bicycles are carried free with a Rover ticket. Another option is to purchase the **CalMac Island Hopscotch** ticket, available for use on 26 routes and valid for 30 days unlimited travel on each route. For example, a ticket for the Oban–Lochboisdale–Berneray–Leverburgh–Stornoway–Ullapool route allows you to visit South and North Uist, Harris and Lewis and costs £23.70 per passenger and £111 per car. See the CalMac guide or call the numbers above for full details.

Getting around

You should allow plenty of time to explore the islands fully. With your own transport and travelling from top to bottom, a week would be enough time for a whistle-stop tour but not enough to explore in any depth or scratch beneath the surface. You will need to allow for the lack of public transport on Sundays on most islands (taxi is the only way around), and for the fact that weather conditions (including the tide at Barra airport) can occasionally affect ferry and flight timetables.

Air Flybe/Loganair ① *www.flybe.com, T0871-700 2000,* fly daily between Barra, Benbecula and Stornoway.

Bus Bus services have improved and now run regularly to most main towns and villages on the islands (see www.cne-siar.gov.uk).

Never on a Sunday

The islands are the Gaidhealtachd, the land of the Gael. Gaelic culture has remained more prominent here than in any other part of Scotland, and the way of life and philosophy of the islanders will seem totally alien and fascinating to many visitors. Gaelic is the first language for the majority of the islanders – and the only one for the older generation – but the all-pervading influence of the English media has taken its toll and the language is under threat. Though Gaelic is still taught in schools, the younger generation tends to speak to each other in English. Visitors will not have any language problems, as the Gaelic- speaking inhabitants are so polite they will always change to English when visitors are present (though place names and signposts are in Gaelic).

The church is also an important factor in preserving the language, and services are usually held in Gaelic. In fact, religion is one of the most pervasive influences on Hebridean life, and the islanders' faith is as strong as the winds that pound their shores. The islands are split between the Presbyterian Lewis, Harris and North Uist, and the predominantly Roman Catholic South Uist and Barra. Benbecula, meanwhile, has a foot in both camps.

On Lewis and Harris the Free Church is immensely powerful and the Sabbath is strictly observed. Don't expect to travel anywhere by public transport; shops and petrol stations will be closed, and you'll be hard pressed to find a place to eat. Even the swings in the playgrounds are padlocked! Things are changing, however, and October 2002 saw the revolutionary move to allow Loganair to fly to Stornoway on a Sunday. Despite a tsunami-like wave of protest from the church, who described the idea as "a breach of God's moral law", Loganair's tourist-friendly flights took to the air.

Car Most of the islands' roads are single track but in good condition and, unlike other parts of the Highlands and Islands, not too busy though you may encounter a road blocked by cattle and wandering sheep! On Sunday you'll barely meet another soul. Petrol stations are few and far between, expensive and closed on Sundays so if low on petrol think carefully before passing a fuel sign. The normal rules for single track roads apply and, as elsewhere in the Highlands, you need to look out for sheep. Distances are greater than most people imagine. For example, the distance from Nis (Ness) at the northern tip of Lewis to Leverburgh in the south of Harris is 85 miles. From Stornoway to Tarbert is 37 miles. And the distance from Otternish in the north of North Uist to Lochboisdale, the main ferry port on South Uist, is 50 miles. Several local car hire agencies offer reasonable rental deals. Expect to pay around £30 per day, depending on the size of engine and age of the car. You cannot take a rented car off the islands.

Cycle Cycling is a great way to explore the islands. You can fully appreciate the amazing scenery around, and it only costs a few pounds to transport a bike by ferry. There is, of course, the major problem of strong winds, which can leave you frustrated and exhausted, especially if cycling into the prevailing south-westerly wind. ▶ *For further details, see Transport pages 71, 80 and 94.*

Ferry A ferry sails to Berneray from Leverburgh (Harris) at least three times daily. Several ferries sail daily from Barra to the island of Eriskay. There's also a regular passenger ferry from Ludag in South Uist to Eoligarry on Barra.

Tourist information

There are tourist information centres in Stornoway and Tarbert, which are open all year, and also in Lochmaddy, Lochboisdale and Castlebay, which are open early April to mid October. Full details are given under each destination. **Visit Hebrides** ⓘ *www.visithebrides. com*, produces an accommodation brochure and TIC's also stock the free and handy *Explore the Outer Hebrides Guide with Maps*, which details key routes and places of interest. The Visit Hebrides website also provides lots of information on the islands, including accommodation and up-and-coming events. You should invest in a copy of the *Highlands & Islands Travel Guide*, which is available from the local TICs. Accommodation on the islands is generally not difficult to find, except perhaps at the height of the summer when you should book in advance, either directly or through the local tourist office. It's also a good idea to book ahead if you're staying on a Sunday, and if you're staying in the countryside you should check if there's a convenient pub or hotel to eat in. Certainly, as highlighted by the recent formation of the **Outer Hebrides Speciality Food Trail** ⓘ *www.foodhebrides. com*, you won't go hungry on these islands, which are renowned for the quality of their seafood, meat and real ale. There are many excellent self-catering options on the islands and this is a most cost-effective way to get to know one particular island. Check out the Visit Hebrides website, see above.

Activities

Those intent on walking in the islands should visit the excellent website walking. visitscotland.com, which has details of over 18 walks in the Hebrides. Several operators offer guided walking holidays, see Essentials, page 57, for further details. A great way to experience the islands is to get out onto the water, and in addition to excellent wildlife cruises, don't forget that the Outer Hebridean chain is now regarded as one of Europe's best locations for sea kayaking (see **Uist Outdoor Centre (www.uistoutdoorcentre. co.uk)** and **Clearwater Paddling (www.clearwaterpaddling.com)**, page 93). If surfing's your thing then you're also in the right place. The northwest coast of Lewis, especially the stretch between Dalmore Bay and the beach at Barabhas, has some of the best surfing in Britain.

Leodhas (Lewis)

Lewis constitutes the northern two thirds of the most northerly island in the Outer Hebrides. It is by far the most populous of the Outer Hebridean islands and, with over 20,000 inhabitants, makes up two thirds of the total population. Just over 8000 people live in and around Stornoway, the largest town in the Hebrides and the administrative capital of the Western Isles. The majority of the rest of the population live in over 280 crofting townships strung out along the west coast between Port Nis (Ness) and Càrlabhagh (Carloway). The west coast is also where you'll find the island's most interesting sight: the prehistoric remains of Dùn Chàrlabhaigh (Carloway) Broch, the impressive Calanais (Callanish) Standing Stones, the restored blackhouse village of Garenin and the Arnol Blackhouse. These can all be visited as a day trip from Stornoway, either on an organized tour or on the 'West Side Circular' bus service. The interior of the northern half is flat peat bog, hence the island's name which means 'marshy' in Gaelic. Further south, where Lewis becomes Harris, the scenery is more dramatic as the relentlessly flat landscape gives way to rocky hills, providing the backdrop to the sea lochs that cut deep into the coast and the beautiful beaches around Uig. Look out for a free copy of the leaflet *Outdoor Hebrides* at TIC's.» *For listings, see pages 68-71.*

Background

Lewis was controlled by the Vikings and the Norse influence can be seen in many of the place names, such as Uig (which is Norse for 'a bay'). After the end of Norwegian sovereignty in 1266, the island was ruled by the Macleods, said to be descendants of early settlers from Iceland. Control of the island was wrested from them by the Mackenzies, who then proceeded to sell it, in 1844, to Sir James Matheson. The new owner built Lews Castle in Stornoway and began to develop the infrastructure of the island, as well as investing in new industries. Though many crofts were cleared and families sent to Canada, the people of Lewis fared well and certainly much better than their counterparts in the Southern Isles.

The next proprietor was Lord Leverhulme, founder of Lever Brothers, who bought the island (along with Harris) in 1918. He planned to turn Lewis into a major fishing centre and ploughed money into developing the infrastructure. He was forced to abandon his plans, however, partly because of the decline of the fishing industry, and partly owing to the growing conflict between him and the islanders returning from the war who wanted land of their own to farm. As a final benevolent gesture, Lord Leverhulme offered Lewis to the islanders, but only Stornoway Council accepted. The island was then divided into estates and sold, and hundreds of people emigrated.

Today the economy of Lewis is still based on the traditional industries of crofting, fishing and weaving, though there are other economic activities such as fish farming, which is now a major employer, service industries, construction, the controversial wind farm development and increasingly, tourism.

Steòrnabhagh (Stornoway) → *For listings, see pages 68-71. Phone code 01851.*

The fishing port of Stornoway, the only town in the Outer Hebrides, is the islands' commercial capital and, as such, boasts more services and facilities than you might expect in any town of comparable size. It's not a pretty place, dominated as it is by the oil industry, but has the full range of banks, shops, hotels, guesthouses, pubs and restaurants, garages, car hire firms, sports facilities, an airport and ferry terminal, and, for the visiting tourist, it presents a rare opportunity to stock up on supplies.

Stornoway is also the administrative capital and home to the Comhairle nan Eilean (Western Isles Council), which has done much to broaden the local economy and to promote and protect Gaelic language and culture. The BBC is rapidly developing programmes and a digital network dedicated to the Gaelic language. Indeed, every July, Stornoway and the Hebridean islands host the **Hebridean Celtic Festival** ① *www. hebceltfest.com*, an ever expanding and popular celebration of Celtic music and the arts that also attracts international acts.

Ins and outs

Getting there and around Stornoway is the island's transport hub. The airport is 4 miles east of the town centre, a £6 taxi ride away. **Flybe/Loganair** ① *T0871-700 2000, www.fly be.com*, flies from Glasgow to Stornoway twice a day from Monday to Saturday. There is a also a daily flight from Edinburgh and four flights a day from Inverness. The CalMac ferry terminal is just beyond the bus station, which is on South Beach, a short walk from the town centre. CalMac runs a ferry service from Ullapool to Stornoway, two or three times a day in the summer and twice daily in the winter, Monday to Saturday. A one-way ticket costs £7.85 per passenger and £39.50 per car. Contact the CalMac offices ① *T01854-612358*, in Ullapool for further details. Buses leave from Stornoway to all parts of the island, see page 71, for further details. Note that buses do not run on Sunday. It is advisable to pick up a free copy of the comprehensive Lewis and Harris bus timetables at the TIC, or visit www.cne-siar.gov.uk.

The town is compact and most of what you need is within easy walking distance of the tourist office. Some of the B&Bs in the residential areas are quite a distance from the centre, but there's an hourly town bus service, or hire a taxi. ➡ *For further details, see Transport, page 71.*

Tourist information The helpful **TIC** ① *26 Cromwell St, T01851-703088, Easter-Sep Mon-Sat 0900-1800, Oct-Easter 0900-1700 (though opening hours vary) and for the arrival of the evening ferry* , stocks maps, bus timetables and various books and brochures. It also sells tickets for minibus tours to Calanais, and wildlife trips around Lewis and Harris.

Sights

Stornoway is short on conventional tourist sights and once you've been to the tourist office and bought the necessities from the local supermarkets, there's not much else to do. The focal point of the town has always been its sheltered deep-water **harbour** and, though the fishing industry has declined since its peak at the end of the last century, there's still a fair amount of activity in the early morning as the latest fresh catch is loaded onto trucks

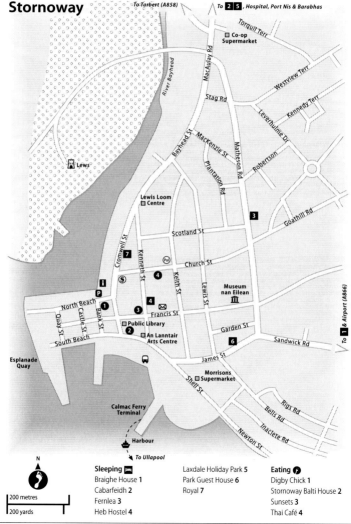

Stornoway

To Tarbert (A858)

To 2 5 , Hospital, Port Nis & Barabhas

Sleeping		Laxdale Holiday Park 5	Eating
Braighe House 1		Park Guest House 6	Digby Chick 1
Cabarfeidh 2		Royal 7	Stornoway Balti House 2
Fernlea 3			Sunsets 3
Heb Hostel 4			Thai Café 4

for far-flung European destinations. On a Saturday morning you can buy the latest fresh batch of fish from a market stall on Point Street by the town hall. The harbour is usually full of seals, giving the town its nickname of Portrona (port of seals). There's a good view across the harbour to **Lews Castle**, a 19th-century edifice built by Sir James Matheson with money earned from opium and tea. The castle now houses a college and its real attraction is the wooded grounds, the only place you'll see trees on the islands.

Museum nan Eilean ① *Francis St, T01851-709266, Apr-Sep Mon-Sat 1000-1730, Oct-Mar Tue-Fri 1000-1700, Sat 1000-1300, free,* features a range of temporary exhibitions on island life and history. Anyone remotely interested in Harris Tweed should visit the **Lewis Loom Centre** ① *T01851-704500, Mon-Sat 1000-1700, £2.50,* housed in the Old Grainstore at the northern end of Cromwell Street, just off Bayhead. The 40-minute guided tour includes demonstrations of traditional methods of warping, dyeing and spinning, and offers a detailed history of Harris Tweed. There's also a craft shop.

The **An Lanntair Arts Centre** ① *T01851-703307, www.lanntair.com, Mon-Sat 1000-late, free,* is the main venue for social and cultural events on the islands. The light and airy building has exhibition spaces for local, national and international artists, a cinema, and stages for various musical and theatrical events. There's also a very good café (see Eating, page 70).

North to Nis (Ness) → *For listings, see pages 68-71.*

The A857 leaves Stornoway and runs northwest through barren, treeless and relentlessly bleak moorland to **Barabhas (Barvas)**. The landscape is scarred by deep gashes caused by peat digging, and the unfamiliar smell you detect in your nostrils is peat burning – a strange mixture of burning grass, whisky and coffee. Peat is the main source of domestic fuel used on the islands, and outside most houses you'll see large stacks of peat, or *cruachs*.

The road from Barabhas northeast to Nis runs through a series of forlorn-looking, scrawny settlements that all seem identical and merge into one. They consist of modern, characterless grey pebble-dash cottages with the ubiquitous piles of peat in the gardens; the abandoned cars and vans scattered around everywhere only add to the ugly and depressing scene.

Just beyond Barabhas a sign points left to the **Morvern Art Gallery**, which has a café, making it a welcome refuge in bad weather. A few miles further on is a turning right to **Baile an Trùiseil (Ballantrushel)**, site of the huge **Clach an Trùiseil**, a 20-ft monolith (the largest in Europe), which was the scene of the last major battle on the island, fought between the Morrisons of Nis and the MacAuleys of Uig. This is the first of a number of prehistoric sights between here and **Siadar (Shader)**, which may be of interest to the keen archaeologist. Otherwise there's little of note on the road north to Nis as it passes through the typical crofting townships of **Coig Peighinnean Buirgh (Five Penny Borve)**, **Gàbhsann bho Dheas (South Galson)**, **Dail (Dell)**, **Suainebost (Swainbost)**, **Tàbost (Habost)** and **Lìonal (Lionel)**. In saying that, those who are keen to buy souvenirs should look in at the **Borgh Pottery** ① *T01856-850345, Mon-Sat 0930-1800, www.borghpottery.com,* by the bridge at Coig Peighinnean. Here you'll find a wide range of beautiful and original domestic and decorative ware.

The road continues north, passing through a number of villages that collectively make up **Nis (Ness)**, until it ends at the fishing village of **Port Nis (Port of Ness)**. It's a lovely spot, with a picturesque little harbour, and a golden sweep of beach enclosed by steep cliffs. Each September the locals head out to the island of **Sula Sgeir**, 30 miles to the north, for the annual cull of young gannets (*gugas*), which are considered something of a delicacy by the people of Lewis (but be warned: they're an acquired taste). In Ness, the kids will love the community established play park set amidst the machair and dunes.

Croft conversion

The word 'croft' is derived from the Gaelic croit, meaning a small area of land. Crofting has been the traditional way of life in the Scottish Highlands for many centuries. Its emotive hold on the psyche of the Highlander comes from the long, hard struggle for security of tenure.

A croft is aptly described as a parcel of land entirely surrounded by regulations. Most crofts consist of a few acres of arable land with a proportion of grazing land shared with other crofts. Each crofter is, in effect, a kind of small tenant-farmer, the distinction being that he has almost absolute security of tenure and has the right to assign the croft to a member of his family whether the landlord agrees or not. In fact, over the years, the crofter has managed to acquire most of the rights of ownership with few of the disadvantages.

The croft is the area of land involved and not the house which is called the 'croft house'. Crofts can vary in size, from a quarter of an acre upwards. Those on Lewis are small and relatively unproductive, with an average size of only about 5 acres, while on the Uists, where the land is more fertile, crofts are up to 50 acres or more.

As well as having the sole tenancy of the croft, the crofter usually has a share in a huge area of 'common grazing' along with the other members of the crofting community – commonly called a township. They also work together in such activities as fencing, sheep dipping or cutting peat.

In reality, crofting does not provide a viable means of living. Very few crofters rely solely on their smallholding for an income and most need to have several occupations (including running a B&B) to make ends meet. But without the family croft, whole communities would just pack up and leave, so crofting functions as a means of preventing the depopulation of remote rural areas.

The crofter's lot may change for the better, however, thanks to the Scottish Parliament's new Land Reform Bill, which includes a special right to buy for the crofting communities.

Just before Port Nis is Lìonal, where the B8015 turns off right and leads to the start of the 10-mile coastal trail to **Tòlstadh (Tolsta North)** and the beautiful beaches of Traigh Mhor and Garry. Numerous shielings (basic stone huts where farming communities lived during summer grazings in high pasture) pepper the landscape from an earlier era when local crofters drove their cattle to the summer pastures in the island's interior. The beaches can be reached much more easily by road north from Stornoway. For details of the coastal walk, ask at the tourist information centre in Stornoway.

Another minor road heads northwest to the tiny hamlet of **Eòropaidh (Eoropie)** (pronounced 'Yor-erpee'). By the road junction that leads to Rubha Robhanais is the ancient **Teampull Mholuaidh (St Moluag's Church)**, thought to date from the 12th century and restored to its present state in 1912. It is now used on certain Sundays by Stornoway's Episcopal Church. From Eòropaidh a narrow road runs to the lighthouse at **Rubha Robhanais (Butt of Lewis)**, the most northerly tip of the island. It's a great place for spotting seabirds or whales and dolphins, but also very wild and windy. Half a mile back down the road a path leads to the tiny beach of **Port Sto**, which is more sheltered.

The west coast of Lewis contains most of what you'll want to see and can be covered in a day trip from Stornoway, either with your own transport, by public bus or as part of a minibus tour.

Arnol

At the end of the village of Arnol is the **Blackhouse Museum** ① *T01851-710395 (HS), Apr-Sep Mon-Sat 0930-1730, Oct-Mar Mon-Sat 0930-1630, £4, concessions £3.20, children £2.40* , one of the best surviving examples of an original blackhouse in Scotland and well worth visiting. These traditional thatched houses were once common throughout the Highlands and Islands, and were inhabited until the 1960s. They were built in the tradition of 'longhouses', which can be traced back 1000 years to the time of the Viking invaders. The name 'blackhouse' dates back to the 1850s when modern buildings were introduced. These were known as 'white houses' so the older-style houses were called 'blackhouses'. The blackhouses were well adapted to the harsh local climate. They had no windows or chimney and were built with local materials – stone, turf and thatch of oat, barley or marram grass – with a peat fire burning continually in the central hearth. Attached to the living quarters was the cattle byre. This particular blackhouse was built in 1885 and inhabited until 1964.

Siabost and around

Two miles south of the Arnol turn-off, at **Bragar**, look out for an archway, formed from the jawbone of a blue whale that was washed up on the coast nearby in 1920. A few miles further on is the township of Siabost (Shawbost), where the charmingly ramshackle **folk museum** ① *Apr-Sep Mon-Sat 0900-1800, free*, which was started as a project by local school- children, now contains an interesting collection of Hebridean artefacts.

Just south of Siabost, beside a small loch, is the sign for the recently restored **Norse Mill and Kiln**, which are a half-mile walk over the hill from the car park. There's not much to see as yet, but it's worth getting out of the car if you want to stretch your legs. A little further on is the popular surfing beach at Dalmore before you reach the turning for **Dail Beag** (**Dalbeg**), another lovely secluded beach.

Gearrannan (Garenin)

The landscape gradually becomes more undulating and scenically interesting as the road then passes through the village of **Càrlabhagh** (**Carloway**), Lord Leverhume's proposed fishing port. Here, a branch road leads to the ruined and deserted blackhouse village of Gearrannan (Garenin). Since 1989, the old village has been extensively renovated, with the aid of EU funding, and several derelict crofts have been painstakingly restored to their original style of stone walls and thatched roofs. One of these is now a **museum** ① *T01851- 643416, Apr-Sep Mon-Sat 0930-1730, £3, concessions £2*. There's also a Gatliff Trust hostel (see Sleeping, page 74), called **Garenin Hostel**, a café serving snacks and light lunches, and four self-catering cottages. An old cart track leads down to the bay, from where the sight of the sun setting out at sea really is something to behold. Above the village, a 4-mile coastal footpath can be followed through the lazy beds (see page 77) and above the sea cliffs to reveal a stunning view of beautiful **Dalmore Bay**. The Atlantic waves seem to break relentlessly on golden sands and the beach is, not surprisingly, a favourite haunt of surfers from Stornoway and further afield. Swimmers and bathers should be careful, however, because, as with many of the west coast beaches, there can be a fierce rip-current carrying the unwary into deeper water out at sea. Ask at

Gatliff Trust

The **Gatliff Hebridean Hostels Trust** (**GHHT**) is a non-profit-making charitable organization run entirely by volunteers, working with the island community to establish, maintain and develop a chain of 'value-for-money' hostels offering clean, cheap, simple, safe, welcoming and traditional croft-style accommodation in dramatic and beautiful locations for visitors to the Outer Hebrides.

The GHHT is independent of the SYHA but has adopted status. Visitors do not have to be members of either organization to use and stay in the hostels. First established in 1961 by Herbert Gatliff, the trust was originally intended to provide young persons of limited means with the opportunity to meet local people and enjoy the unique natural environment and cultural heritage of the islands. However, in recent years, visitors of all incomes, ages, nationalities and interests have been encouraged to use the facilities.

The trust is currently involved in the operation of four hostels situated at **Garenin** (Isle of Lewis), **Rhenigidale** (Isle of Harris), **Berneray** (North Uist) and **Howmore** (South Uist). Further hostels may be opened on other islands in the future.

The hostels are open all year and looked after by non-resident wardens who live and practise crofting nearby. No advance bookings are accepted but it is very unlikely that visitors will find themselves turned away and without a bed for the night. There is also limited space for camping at the hostels. Hostels provide bunk/camp beds, cooking facilities and cutlery, piped water, toilets and coal/wood fires, but visitors should bring their own food and a sleeping bag is recommended.

Current charges are: £8 per night, under 18s £5.50, camping £4.50, day visitors £1. Annual membership £10, under 18s £7.50. For further information regarding membership, contact details, hostel locations and photographs, a reading list and places of interest to visit in the surrounding area, visit the GHHT website, www.gatliff.org.uk.

the Gearrannan village, where you can also stay in unique blackhouse accommodation (see Sleeping, page 75), for a map of this coastal walking route that ends in Dalbeg.

Dùn Chàrlabhaigh (Doune Carloway) Broch

A little further on, standing a few hundred yards from the main road, is the Dùn Chàrlabhaigh Broch (Dun Carloway), the best-preserved building of its type in the Outer Hebrides. The impressive 2000-year-old drystone habitation is beautifully situated on a rocky outcrop, commanding great views across Loch Carloway to the sea beyond. The remaining outer wall is 30-ft high and slopes inwards, with an inner wall which rises vertically, leaving chambers between the walls. Parts of the inner wall have collapsed, revealing the interior stairs and galleries. The **Doune Broch Visitor Centre** ⓘ *T01851-643338, Apr-Oct Mon-Sat 1000-1800, free*, which can be found here, tastefully complements the architectural style of the site, and which gives a good audio-visual description of how life must have been in one of these structures around 50 BC. There's also a small shop and public toilets.

Calanais (Callanish)

ⓘ *www.calanaisvisitorcentre.co.uk, T01851-621422 (HS), site open Apr-Sep daily 1000-1900, Oct-Mar daily 1000-1600, free, visitor centre is open Apr-Sep Mon-Sat 1000-1800, Oct-Mar Wed-Sat 1000-1600.*

Music to your ears

As the heartland of Gaelic culture, the Outer Hebrides are host to many music events throughout the year ranging from a spontaneous ceilidh to one of the three local mods. Mods usually consist of three days of competition in piping, singing, instrumental music, drama and poetry, and are an opportunity to see the best of the local talent. More information can be obtained from An Comunn Gaidhealach, T01851-703487.

Also listed below are the various Highland Games and agricultural shows, where you can also see piping competitions and Highland dancing.

Late March Feis nan Coisir, Stornoway, Lewis.

First Friday in April Donald Macleod Memorial Piping Competition, Stornoway, Lewis.

May-June Highland Festival, held in various locations.

Early June Harris Mod, Tarbert, on Harris.

Second week in June Lewis Mod, Stornoway, Lewis.

Mid June Uist Mod, Iochdar, on South Uist.

May-June Lochmaddy Boat Festival, Lochmaddy, North Uist.

Mid July Berneray Week, Bearnaraigh (Berneray), North Uist.

July Ceolas Music School, South Uist.

Early July Barra Festival for two weeks.

Early/mid July Feis Tir an Eorna, Paibeil, North Uist; Barra Highland Games, Borgh (Borve), Barra, lasting for a week.

11-14 July Hebridean Celtic Music Festival, Stornoway, Lewis.

Mid July North Uist Highland Games, Hosta, North Uist.

Mid/late July Harris Gala; South Uist Highland Games, Aisgeirnis (Askernish), South Uist; Lewis Highland Games, Tong, Lewis.

Mid July Barra Highland Games.

Third week of July Harris Festival

Late July Barra Live, Barra; West Side Agricultural Show, Barabhas (Barvas), Lewis; South Uist Agricultural Show, Iochdar, South Uist; South Harris Agricultural Show, Leverburgh.

July Feis Eilean an Fhraoich, Stornoway, Lewis.

Late July/early August North Uist Agricultural Show, Hosta, North Uist.

Early August Carloway Agricultural Show, Càrlabhagh (Carloway), Lewis; Fies Tir a Mhurain, Lionacleit, Benbecula; Lewis Carnival, Stornoway; Fish Festival, Stornoway; Twin Peaks Hill Race, North Uist.

Second week August Harris Arts Festival, Tarbert.

Five miles south of Dun Chàrlabhaigh is the jewel in the islands' prehistoric crown, and one of the most atmospheric and evocative places in Scotland, if not the UK. The **Calanais Standing Stones** are the equal of Stonehenge in historical value but what sets them apart is their imposing physical presence, which can be appreciated at close quarters, and their spectacularly beautiful setting. The stones are aligned in the form of a Celtic cross and, in the centre, is a main circle of 13 stones, with a central monolith over 12-ft tall, and a chambered burial cairn. The oldest part of this great ceremonial site – probably the stone circle – dates from around 3000 BC (older than Stonehenge) and continued in use until about 800 BC. The full significance of the site is not yet known, though it is thought to be a lunar calendar, built to track the path of the lunar cycle. Every 18.6 years the moon returns to the same point and the stones at Calanais plot its slow progress over the intervening years until the moon 'sets' inside the stone circle. This astounding event – known as a lunar standstill – last occurred in 2006. There are also a number of smaller and more isolated stone circles a few miles south of Calanais on the road to Gearraidh na h-Aibhne (Garynahine). Next to the stones is the **Calanais**

Visitor Centre, which features 'The Story of the Stones' exhibition, a very good restaurant (see Eating, page 70) and a shop. Margaret Curtis, who has been studying and excavating the site for over 30 years, offers a guided archaeological tour (see Activities and tours, page 70).

The Uig Peninsula → *For listings, see pages 68-71.*

From Gearraidh na h-Aibhne the main A858 runs back to Stornoway, while the B8011 forks west to the remote Uig Peninsula in the southwest of the island. Here are some of the Outer Hebrides' finest beaches and most dramatic coastal scenery, and you'll barely see another soul.

Bearnaraigh (Great Bernera) to Cnip

Four miles down this road is a turning to the right onto the B8059, which leads to the island of Bearnaraigh, now connected to the mainland of Lewis by a single-track road bridge. The main settlement on the island is **Breacleit (Breaclete)**, where you can find out about the island's history and the Iron Age village at Bostadh from the **Bernera Museum** ① *T01851-612285, Jun-Sep Mon-Sat 1100-1800, £2.* The rest of the island is fairly interesting with tiny fishing villages, one or two brochs and some standing stones. The nicest part, though, is on the north coast, near the tiny hamlet of **Bostadh (Bosta)**, where a lovely little sandy bay looks out to the nearby island of **Bearnaraigh Beag (Little Bernera)**.

The B8011 continues across bleak moorland, then cuts north to **West Loch Roag**, which is fringed by some fine sandy beaches and backed by a much hillier landscape. Just beyond **Miabhag (Miavaig)** is the turn-off right to **Cliobh (Cliff)**, with its picturesque beach which is unsafe for swimming. A mile further on is the little village of **Cnip (Kneep)**, to the east of which is the beautiful **Traigh na Berie**, a long sandy beach backed by flat machair which is ideal for camping.

Gallan Head

Beyond Miabhag, the eerie peninsula of Gallan Head provides a setting befitting a science fiction drama or Cold War Orwellian novel, with empty, decaying Ministry of Defence buildings battered by the Atlantic storms. Wandering around the abandoned site, it is easy to form ideas of bizarre, top-secret government experiments and early-warning missile tracking in this seemingly edge-of-the-world place, far removed from the unwanted, prying eyes of everyday society.

Mangersta and the Flannan Islands

Beyond Ardroil the road continues to Mangersta where, at Aird Fenish, is some of the most spectacular coastal scenery in the Outer Hebrides. The cliffs plunge dramatically beyond the road to the inaccessible beach below, with a series of crumbling sea stacks battered by the fearsome waves, and seabirds riding the updraughts adding to the sense of natural beauty, energy and sheer power. Further south at **Brenish**, about a 10-minute walk from the road, is a menacing blowhole connected to the sea by an underground passage.

Far out into the Atlantic are the haunting Flannan Islands, scene of an unsolved mystery in 1900 following the disappearance of three lighthouse keepers. Various explanations have been put forward over the years, ranging from a freak wave in stormy weather to a monster sea serpent or even a dispute and fight between the men; whatever the real reason, the legend continues. See page 70 for boat trips.

Timsgearraidh (Timsgarry)

At Timsgearraidh (Timsgarry) are the **Traigh Chapadail (Uig sands)** at the village of **Eadar Dha Fhadhail (Adroil)**. This is the loveliest of all the beaches on Lewis, with miles of sand dunes and machair, but it is famous for an entirely different reason. It was here in 1831 that a crofter dug up the 'Lewis Chessmen', 78 pieces carved from walrus ivory and belonging to at least eight incomplete chess sets from 12th-century Scandinavia. Some are now in the Museum of Scotland in Edinburgh, but most can be found outside their country of origin, in the British Museum in London (where you'll also find the Elgin Marbles). In recent years the Scottish Government has reportedly made several requests to the British Museum for the return of the chessmen.

Leodhas (Lewis) listings

For Sleeping and Eating price codes and other relevant information, see pages 12-19.

● Sleeping

For those who want to visit the South Lochs on the east of Lewis, there are a couple of accommodation options: **Tigh Na Bruaich (££)**, 8 Balallan, off the A859 miles from Stornoway, T01851-830742, T07763-185281, a traditional croft house; and **Kershader Hostel (£)**, on the south shore of Loch Erisort off the A859 near North Harris, T01851-880236, www.syha.org.uk, cosy community-run 14-bed hostel with great facilities including a café and knitwear shop, ideal for accessing local birdwatching, fishing and walking.

Stornoway *p60, map p61*

As the largest settlement on the islands, Stornoway has a good selection of accommodation from which to choose, though you should book in advance in the peak summer season. The TIC will do this for you, for a small fee. There are many B&Bs in and around the town centre, some of which offer a 'room only' rate, including on Matheson Rd close to the town centre and ferry terminal.

£££ Cabarfeidh Hotel, Perceval Rd South, T01851-702604, www.cabarfeidh-hotel. co.uk. 46 rooms. On the outskirts of town and not as convenient as the **Royal**. Free broadband and all modern trappings.

£££ Royal Hotel, Cromwell St, T01851-702109, www.royalstornoway.co.uk. 26 rooms.

Billed as Stornoway's most historic hotel, great value, central and with views across the marina. Reasonable food in its contemporary, all wood HS-1 café-bar, but for atmosphere and a tremendous meal book a table in its **Boatshed** restaurant (see Eating, below).

££ Braighe House, 20 Braighe Rd, T01851-705287, www.braighehouse.co.uk. Open all year. Four en suite rooms. Very comfortable, tastefully furnished accommodation in modern house with sea views. Tasty breakfasts and friendly welcome. A good alternative to the more expensive hotels in town. Recommended.

££-£ Park Guest House, 30 James St, T01851-702485. 8 rooms. This Victorian townhouse is comfortable, only 500 yds from the ferry terminal, and is the best of the guesthouses. It also has an excellent restaurant. Price is **££** with dinner, **£** for room only.

££-£ Fernlea, 9 Matheson Rd, T01851-702125, www.fernlea-guesthouse.co.uk Open Feb-Dec. Recently upgraded Victorian listed building with 3 en suite rooms. Room only **£**. Off-street parking.

£ Heb Hostel, 25 Kenneth St, Stornoway, T01851-709889, www.hebhostel.com. Centrally located hostel with 26 beds. Clean and friendly.

£ Laxdale Holiday Park, Laxdale Lane, about a mile out of town on the road to Barabhas, T01851-703234, www. laxdaleholidaypark.com. Open all year. Bunkhouse has 16 beds and good facilities, including showers and toilets suitable for the disabled. The park also has space for 37 tents (£7 per night), and a 3-bedroom self-catering bungalow (from £350 per week).

North to Nis *p62*

£££ Broad Bay House, Back, Lewis, T01851-820990, wwwbroadbayhouse.co.uk. About 9 miles north of Stornoway. Modern and recently opened luxurious 4-bedroom guesthouse overlooking the sea. Beautifully appointed rooms and the opportunity to relax over a delicious 4-course evening meal (♙♙♙ (£35 per person)).

££ Galson Farm Guest House and Bunk-house, Gàbhsann bho Deas (South Galson), halfway between Barabhas and Port Nis, T01851-850492, www.galsonfarm.co.uk. Open all year. Friendly and beautifully restored 18th-century house with sea views. Dinner available (£25pp) (♙♙♙). Owners also have **Galson Farm Bunkhouse** (**£**), which is a small welcoming hostel with 8 beds and basic facilities.

£ Loch Beag B&B, 19 Fivepenny, Ness T01851-810405 This harled bungalow doesn't look much but it's good value for money and closeness to the Traigh sands.

West coast of Lewis *p64*

If you want to stay near the stones and visit them at dusk or sunrise, there are several inexpensive B&Bs in and around the village of Calanais.

££ Cean Bodiach B&B, 10 Tolsta Chaolis, T01851-621722, www.hebrideanholiday cottages.co.uk. Located between the stones and the broch,

££ Leumadiair Guest House, 7a Callanish, T01851-621706, www.leumadair.co.uk. Has views of the stones which are just 2 mins away. It offers a 3-course dinner (£25 per person).

££ Loch Roag and Eshcol Guest House, 21 Breasclete, T01851-621357, www.eshcol. com. Open Mar-Oct. 3 rooms. A few miles from the stones. Comfortable accommodation in modern house overlooking Loch Roag and with the option of a 5-course dinner (♙♙♙).

££ Loch Roag Guest House, T01851-621357, 22a Beascleit, www.lochroag.com.

Open Mar-Oct. 6 rooms. Donald owns the house next door to his father (hence the same telephone number). He also offers high-quality accommodation and dinner, whilst the 2 cedar lodges – with spa – can be let for £800+ a week.

£ Garenin Hostel, Garenin, near Carloway, www.gatliff.org.uk. 1 of 4 Gatliff Trust hostels in the Outer Hebrides (see box, page 65). A renovated blackhouse, situated by a gorgeous beach and with the added benefit of a ground-source heat pump, making it awfully cosy in cold weather. No telephone or TV. Recommended.

Self-catering

£££ Gearrannan Blackhouse Village, Carloway, T01851-643416, www.gearrannan. com. Open all year. 4 blackhouses have been restored and refurbished as self-catering thatched cottages in a fantastic location. One of the cottages sleeps up to 16. Prices from £89 per night.

Great Bernera to Cnip *p67*

£££ Auberge Carnish, 5 Carnish, Uig, T01851-672459, www.aubergecarnish.co.uk. 5-star accommodation and food in a stunning setting, this new venture, run by the couple who formerly owned the acclaimed Bonaventure (now Gallan Head Hotel) opens in May 2011.

£££ Baile Na Cille Guest House, Timsgarry, T01851-672242, www.bailenacille.co.uk. Open Easter-Oct. 7 en suite rooms. One of the best places to stay around Uig bay, this restored 18th-century manse is beautifully located overlooking a 2-mile stretch of sand. Superb home cooking 4-course dinner for £30) and one of the warmest welcomes in the islands.

££ Gallan Head Hotel, north of Timsgarry, Aird Uig, T01851-672474, www.gallanhead hotel.co.uk. Open all year (limited in Dec). 5 rooms. This restaurant with rooms is a great place to stay, and eat. Don't be put off by the grim-looking disused military buildings, accommodation here is very comfortable. And the food, with an emphasis on the preparing locally sourced meats and seafish, is excellent.

🍴 Eating

Stornoway *p70, map p61*
The pubs and hotels serve the usual range of bar meals. Note that pubs are closed on Sun and some hotels cater only for residents.

🍴🍴🍴 The Boatshed, in the **Royal Hotel**, see Sleeping, above. Open daily. Fabulous maritime themed setting with the addition of a roaring open fire, wooden table and stone finishings. Recommended as the best of the hotel options. Less upmarket and offering a reasonably priced menu in a contemporary styled setting, is their **HS-1 Café Bar**.

🍴🍴🍴-🍴🍴 Sunsets Restaurant, 26 Francis St, T01851-705862. Terrific option for diners seeking a taste of the freshest seafood and shellfish in town.

🍴🍴 Digby Chick, 5 Bank St, T01851-700026. Open Mon-Sat for lunch and dinner (closes 2100). This contemporary family-run restaurant is a popular local choice and one of the best places in town for seafood.

🍴🍴-🍴 Stornoway Balti House, 24 South Beach, near the bus station, T01851-706116. For your fix of delicious tandoori and balti dishes, pop into this terrific restaurant that also offers takeaway and an express lunch (£6.50).

🍴🍴-🍴 Thai Café, 27 Church St, T01851-701811. Open Mon-Sat until 2300. Few would expect such authentically good Thai cuisine so far north, but it's true. Come and be amazed. The BYO policy also helps keep prices down.

🍴 Ann Lanntair Arts Centre, Kenneth St, Stornoway, T01851-703307. Good for snacks and light lunches in airy surroundings.

North to Nis *p62*
🍴🍴 The Cross Inn, Cross, Nis (Ness), T01851-810151, www.crossinn.com. The Islands' most northerly restaurant serving locally-grazed beef and the catch of the day.

West coast of Lewis *p64*
🍴 Tigh Mealros, a few miles south of the stones, Gearraidh na h-Aibhne, T01851-621333. Closes at 2100. They serve good

local grub in a cosy, relaxed atmosphere, with scallops a speciality.

🍴 Calanais Visitor Centre Café, see page 65. The best place to eat near the stones, offering diners reasonably priced, freshly made soups, salads and home-baking.

The Uig Peninsula *p67*
🍴🍴🍴 Gallan Head Hotel , see Sleeping, above. Restaurant and B&B serving food Mon-Fri 1830-2100. A plentiful 3-course set dinner for £32, catering for vegetarian and gluten free diets.

🛍 Shopping

Stornoway *p60, map p61*
There's a **Tesco** supermarket beside the ferry terminal (closed Sun), and a **Co-op** by the 1st roundabout on the road out to Barabhas. However, for a taste of the Hebrides, pop into some of the following outlets in and around Stornoway: **Hebridean Brewing Company**,18a Bells Rd, www.hebridean-brewery.co.uk, Mon-Fri 0900-1700, for a real ale taste of the Hebrides; **WJ MacDonald**, 5 Francis St, a butcher making the renowned Stornoway black pudding. If you want to catch your own supper **Sportsworld**, 1-3 Francis St, T01851-705464, sells bait and fishing gear all year round.

The Uig Peninsula *p67*
Uig Lodge Smoked Salmon, T01851-672396, www.uiglodge.co.uk. The place to buy smoked salmon.

🎯 Activities and tours

Stornoway *p60, map p61*
Surfing
Lewis Surf Trek, 18a Guershader, T07939-194880, www.lewissurftrek.com. Lewis is excellent for surfing. Whether you want a half- (£25) or full-day (£40) board and wetsuit hire or a full-blown 2-day surf safari (£90 per person), give these guys a call.

Tour operators
Charles Engebret (T01851-702303) leaves from the pontoon next to the Lifeboat station and takes you to the bird colonies of the Shiant Islands.

Galson Motors, T01851-840269, leaves from Stornoway bus station. Day-trips to Calanais. The RSPB (T01851-703296 www.rspb.org.uk) lead a number of guided walks around breeding grounds and migration stop-offs.

Maclennan's Coaches, at the ferry terminal, T01851-706267. Day-trips to Calanais and the Blackhouse.

West coast of Lewis p64
Tour operators
Margaret Curtis, Olcote, New Park, Calanish, T01851-621277, http://www.geo.org/callan.htm#tof. The 1-hr tour of the Callanish site gives an insight into the history and purpose of the stones.

The Uig Peninsula p67
Island Cruising, 1 Erista, Uig, T01851-672381, www.island-cruising.com. For wildlife, diving, birdwatching and live-aboard boat trips as far afield as the Flannan Islands and St Kilda.

Seatrek, Murray MacLeod, 16 Uigean, Uig, T01851-672469, www.seatrek.co.uk. Aboard a high-speed RIB, this operator offers a host of trips, including a 2-hr (1000-1200) easy cruise off Uig during which you'll also check on the seals and lobster pots (£35); a Sea Stack trip off Little Bernera (1300-1500 £35); an island trip with ruins and sea caves (£45); and a full-blown day (£95) that includes the chance to see the isle of Scarp, famous for the film The Rocket Post (see Scarp page 74).

⊖ Transport

Stornoway p60, map p61
Air Flybe/Loganair, T0871-700 2000, www.flybe.com, flies to **Glasgow**, Mon-Sat, 2 daily, 1 hr. There is a daily flight to **Edinburgh**, 1 hr, and flights from **Inverness** Mon-Sat, 4 daily, 40 mins. Eastern Airways

T08703-669100, www.easternairways.com, flies daily to Aberdeen Mon-Fri 55 mins.
Bus From Stornoway to **Port Nis** (**Ness**) via **Barabhas** (**Barvas**), 4-6 times daily; to **Arnol**, **Siabost** (**Shawbost**), **Càrlabhagh** (**Carloway**), **Calanais** (**Callanish**), and back to Stornoway, 'West Side Circular', 4-6 times daily; to **Bear-naraigh** (**Great Bernera**) via **Gearraidh na h-Aibhne** (**Garynahine**), 4 daily; to **Uig District**, 3-4 daily; to **Ranais** (**Ranish**), 6-8 times daily. Contact the tourist office in Stornoway, T01851-703088, or the bus station, T01851-704327, for further details.

There are also buses from Stornoway to **Tarbert** and **Leverburgh** on Harris (for the ferry to North Uist), T01851-705050, 4-5 times daily, Mon-Sat. Bus timetables are available from the tourist office.
Ferry CalMac runs a ferry service to **Ullapool**, 2 times Mon-Sat (Mar-mid Jun) 3 times on Wed (Mid Jun-Aug) and 1 daily Nov-Feb. It also now runs once on a Sun all year round (2 hrs 40 mins). Contact **CalMac** offices in Stornoway, T01851-702361, for further details.
Car and cycle hire Car and bike rental is available at good rates from **Lewis Car Rentals**, 52 Bayhead St, T01851-703760; **Mackinnon Self Drive**, 18 Inaclete Rd, T01851-702984, hires cars; **Alex Dan's Cycle Centre**, 67 Kenneth St, T01851-704025. Mon-Sat 0900-1800, rents bikes for £14 per day and £45 per week.
Taxi Central Cabs, T01851-706900.

West coast of Lewis p64
Car hire/taxi Arnol Car Rentals, Arnol, T01851-710548. Free airport and ferry delivery.

ⓘ Directory

Stornoway p60, map p61
Banks Bank of Scotland, directly opposite the tourist office, has an ATM. Other major banks are also in the centre and also have ATMs. **Internet** Public library, 19 Cromwell St. **Post** Main post office, 16 Francis St.

Na Hearadh (Harris)

Harris is not an island but, together with Lewis, forms the largest of the Outer Hebrides, with Harris taking up the southern third. The two parts are divided by the long sea lochs of Loch Seaforth in the east and Loch Resort in the west, though this division is rarely shown on maps. Though joined, the two are very different in terms of geography. Harris is largely mountain and rock, whereas Lewis is flat moorland. The largest town and site of the ferry terminal is An Tairbeart (Tarbert). To the north are the highest peaks in the Outer Hebrides, surrounded by some of the finest unspoilt wilderness in the whole country. To the south are miles of wonderful beaches; sands and stunning seascapes that will convince you it's the Caribbean. For it's not just the flawless white sand but the gin-clear water that breaks over them. When the sun comes out, it's as if someone had been fiddling with the colour control: cool greens mutate to psychedelic shades of turquoise and blue. The east coast is not so much a contrast as a shock to the system; a preternaturally strange lunar landscape straight out of a science fiction film. With your own transport you could 'do' Harris in a day quite comfortably, but why just spend a day? Whatever the weather, you'll want to spend more time here and appreciate its precious natural beauty. »» *For listings, see pages 77-80.*

Ins and outs → *Phone code 01859.*

Getting there
There's a regular bus service between Stornoway and Tarbert (four to five times a day) Monday to Saturday, which continues to Leverburgh, via the west coast of South Harris. Ferries sail from Uig (Skye) to Tarbert (one hour 35 minutes), once or twice a day, Monday to Saturday. A one-way ticket costs £5.35 per passenger, £24.20 per car. Contact Uig, T01470-542219, or Tarbert, T01859-502444.

Background

The separation of Harris and Lewis dates back to Norse times, when the island was divided between the two sons of Leod, progenitor of the Macleods. Harris remained in

Right to buy

The Forest of Harris is a vast mountain wilderness extending north from West Loch Tarbert to Loch Resort and forming the de facto boundary with Lewis. It is one of the most isolated and unspoilt upland landscapes in Scotland and, because of its remoteness, receives very few visitors. For experienced hillwalkers, however, it is a paradise, offering rugged mountains, dramatic escarpments, airy ridges and desolate glens. There are endless walking possibilities, including a horse- shoe walk around Clisham and a long walk through Glen Ulladale to Kinloch- resort, a former crofting community now abandoned, but once described as the remotest habitation in Britain. Known as the North Harris Estate, this 22,000-acre tract of land was owned and managed by the family of the Bulmer cider empire – until 2003. In a move that had Scottish lairds incandescent with rage, the 800 residents of the estate were granted the right to take over the land on which they live, for more than £2 million, and finally throw off the shackles of feudal rule. Now that they have become masters of their own destiny, the community can relish the thought of a prosperous future, with energy development plans, sporting rights and tourism top of the agenda.

Macleod hands until 1834. The recent history of Harris is closely bound up with that of Lewis. Both were bought by the soap magnate, Lord Leverhulme, see page 59, whose grandiose schemes for Lewis came to nothing. Leverhulme then turned his attentions to Harris, where the peaceful little village of An t-Ob (Obbe) was renamed Leverburgh and transformed into a bustling port with all manner of public works programmes under development. His death in 1925 brought an end to all his plans for Harris and, instead of becoming a town with a projected population of 10,000, Leverburgh reverted to being a sleepy village, with only the harbour, the roads and the change of name to show for it all.

Since the Leverhulme era there has been no main source of employment for the population of 2400 on Harris, though a successful fishing industry continues on Scalpaigh (Scalpay). There is still some crofting supplemented by the acclaimed but financially precarious Harris Tweed industry (www.harristweed.org) though most of the estimated 130 plus Hebridean weavers reside on Lewis. In addition to public services and crafts, tourism is increasingly important to the island. Indeed, with its wealth of Caribbean-like beaches, diversity of wildlife, excellent walking terrain and fabulous accommodation and eating options, this compact Hebridean 'island' is now establishing itself as a year-round destination. The community launched Winter Harris (www.winterharris.com) in 2007 and as a result it's reported that some hoteliers have already seen a 15% rise in profits over the winter months.

Ceann a Tuath na Hearadh (North Harris)

→ For listings, see pages 77-80. Phone code 01859.

North Harris is the most mountainous part of the Outer Hebrides and its wild, rugged peaks are ideal for hillwalking. In 2003, 135,900 acres of the wildlife (including deer) rich former North Harris Estate were purchased for the community for around £8 million to be managed by the North Harris Community Trust. The A859 south from Lewis gets progressively more scenic as it skirts **Loch Siophort (Seaforth)**, and the mountains rise before you like a giant barrier. The road then climbs past **Bogha Glas (Bowglass)** and **Aird** a Mhulaidh (**Ardvourlie**) with **Clisham** (2619 ft), the highest peak in the Outer Hebrides, and **Sgaoth Aird** (1829 ft) towering overhead on either side. Clisham in particular, though not a Munro, is a very staisfying peak to bag: steep, spectacularly craggy and the views from the top will break your heart.

Just off the A859 near Ardvourlie is **Ardvourlie Castle Guest House**. If you can't afford such luxury but still crave the isolation, then carry on south until you reach the turn-off to **Reinigeadal (Rhenigidale)**, which was the most remote community on Harris and accessible only by sea or by a rough hill track until the access road was built. Here you'll find a **Gatliff Trust Youth Hostel**, see Sleeping, page 77. From Reinigeadal an ascent of shapely **Toddun** (528 m) provides exhilarating exercise rewarded with fine views east across the Minch to the mainland and, in the other direction, to the mountain wilderness of North Harris.

The A859 continues west across the crest of the craggy hills then drops down to the turn-off for the single-track B887, which winds its way all the way out to Huisinis (Hushinish) between the impressive mountains of the Forest of Harris on one side and the northern shore of West Loch Tarbert on the other, with views across to the Sound of Taransay and the beaches of South Harris. Immediately beyond the turn-off, you pass through **Bun Abhainn Eadarra (Bunavoneadar)**, which was a thriving whaling station until 1930 and one of Lord Leverhulme's many schemes for the island. The old whaling station is worth a visit even though the site has not been developed as a tourist attraction.

Just before the village of **Miabhag (Meavaig)**, a defined footpath heads north into the hills up Glen Meavaig to Loch Voshimid. Further on, though, is a better opportunity for walking. Just before the gates of **Amhuinnsuidhe Castle** (pronounced 'Avan-soo-ee') is a signpost for Chliostair Power Station. From here you can walk two miles up to the dam, then follow the right-hand track round the reservoir and the left-hand track round the upper loch, before you arrive in a wild and remote glen.

Just beyond the castle gates you'll see a beautiful waterfall spilling straight into the sea. The road then runs right past the front door of the castle, built in 1868 by the Earl of Dunmore, and still a private residence, before passing through an archway and continuing to the tiny crofting township of **Huisinis (Hushinish)**, beautifully situated in a sandy bay. This is where the road ends; next stop the USA. Follow the track to the right across the machair, where a footpath above the jetty and rocky beach can be followed to the old fishing lodge at **Cravadale** and Loch Cravadale beyond. Make a detour to the golden sands and turquoise waters of **Traigh Mheilein**, overlooking Scarp. From the coast, strong walkers can follow Glen Cravadale inland, eventually rejoining the main road near Amhuinnsuidhe Castle.

The rocky island of **Scarp** supported a population of more than 100 as late as the 1940s but was abandoned in 1971, and now the crofters' cottages are used as holiday homes. The island was the scene of a bizarre experiment in 1934, when a German rocket scientist, Gerhard Zucher, tried to prove that rockets could be used to transport mail and medical supplies to remote communities. His theory went up in smoke, however, when the rocket exploded before it even got off the ground, with 30,000 letters on board.

An Tairbeart (Tarbert) and around

→ *For listings, see pages 77-80. Phone code 01859. Population 500.*
Tarbert, the largest settlement on Harris, lies in a sheltered bay on the narrow isthmus that joins North and South Harris. It's a tiny 'capital' but still the main ferry port for the CalMac ferry from Harris to Uig on Skye. Tarbert is also where to find groceries, **Harris**

tweed ⓘ *www.harristweedandknitwear.co.uk*, a post office, petrol, and a range of eating and accommodation options. The TIC ⓘ *T01859-502011, Apr-Oct Mon-Sat 0900-1700 and for the arrival of the evening ferry, in winter check times*, is close to the ferry terminal.

An interesting little excursion from Tarbert is the 10-mile return route that runs east through the tiny villages of **Urgha** and **Caolas Scalpaigh** to **Carnach** at the end of the road. Just beyond Urgha, on the north side of the road, is a path which leads across the hills, part of the land managed by the North Harris Community Land Trust, to the remote settlement of **Reinigeadal**. The twisting path was originally used by the community in Reinigeadal; hardy children would make the daily journey across the hills to Tarbert before the village was connected to the A859 by the new road. The zigzagging, exposed path, on which several people are known to have perished, passes through enchanting scenery above **Loch Trollamarig** in a setting more reminiscent of Scandinavia's fjordland. A visit can easily be made to the deserted village of **Molinginish**, nestled snugly in a small glen above the loch and reputedly where the royal family once anchored for a picnic. Ensure you are properly equipped with boots and rainwear for the 6-mile walk.

The island of **Scalpaigh** (**Scalpay**), now connected to Harris by a road bridge opened by Tony Blair in 1998, is a thriving fishing community with a population of over 400. It's a pleasant three-mile walk across the island to **Eilean Glas Lighthouse**, built by the Stevensons and the first ever on the Outer Hebrides.

Ceann a Deas na Hearadh (South Harris) → *For listings, see pages 77-80.*

An absolute must while you're in the Outer Hebrides is the 45-mile circular route around South Harris. If you only do one thing while you're here, then make sure this is it, for the change in scenery from the west coast to the east is utterly astounding. One thing you're sure to puzzle over as you travel round is the fact that most people live on the harsh and inhospitable east coast, known as Na Baigh (Bays), while the beautiful west coast with its miles of glorious golden sands is scarcely populated. This is not through choice. The fertile west coast housed most of the population until the end of the 18th century when they were cleared to make way for sheep farms. Some emigrated to Cape Breton, while others were 'resettled' by landowners, forced to farm the infertile, rocky soil of the east side.

West coast of Harris
The main road from Tarbert runs south, skirting East Loch Tarbert, then cuts inland and heads west through a dramatic lunar landscape of rocks dotted with tiny lochans. It then begins to descend towards the sea revealing to your right the vast golden expanse of **Losgaintir** (**Luskentyre**) beach. A single-track road turns off to the right and runs out to the tiny settlement of Losgaintir where in his tiny workshop overlooking the machair and azure sea, weaver Donald John Mackay is among the dozen or so Hearrachs (indigenous inhabitants from Harris) who produce the world famous hand-crafted Harris tweed using his loom. The weaver, whom once famously supplied cloth to Nike for a range of training shoes, sells hats (from £12) and hand-woven tweed jackets (from £160) from his workshop at 6 Luskentyre. The road cuts through the rich machair as it follows the magnificent stretch of bleached white sand that fills the entire bay, washed by turquoise sea and backed by steep dunes. All this set against the backdrop of the mountains to the north. This is paradise refrigerated.

A short distance offshore is the island of **Tarasaigh** (**Taransay**), which was well populated at the beginning of the 1900s but was recently abandoned. The island gained national prominence in 2000 as the setting for the popular BBC television series *Castaway*, in which an assortment of supposedly normal people from a variety of backgrounds were challenged to pit their wits against the elements and each other for a period of a full year. You can enjoy a day trip to the island (see Activities and tours, page 79).

The road follows the coast, passing through the tiny settlements of **Seilebost**, **Horgabost** and **Burgh** (**Borve**), Norse names highlighting the Vikings once plundered these lands. At **Horgabost** it's worthwhile making the brief 10-minute stroll above the white sands to marvel at the roughly hewn MacLeod's Stone that overlooks the sea and which dates back to the Bronze Age. There's B&B accommodation at Seilebost and Horgabost, while, a few miles further on, is another beautiful stretch of white sands at **Sgarasta Bheag** (**Scaristabeg**), perfect for surfing, golf and with a couple of stunning places to stay (see Sleeping, page 78).

Beyond Sgarasta Bheag, the village of **An Taobh Tuath** (**Northton**) provides access to the scenic promontory of **Toe Head**, almost cut off from the rest of Harris by the huge expanse of the golden sands at Sgarasta. At the excellent **Seallam Centre** ⓘ *T01859-520258, www.seallam.com, Mon-Sat 1000-1700, £2.50*, you can learn all about the history and natural environment of Harris and take the chance to determine if you have ancestral links to the Hebrides. There's also a lovely café here. Nearby, a ruined chapel of 16th-century origin is situated on the machair below **Chaipaval** (365 m), whose heathery slopes can be climbed for one of the best views out to sea towards St Kilda, some 40 miles distant.

Ant-Ob (Leverburgh)

The road then runs along the south shore until it reaches An t-Ob (formerly Obbe, now Leverburgh), site of Lord Leverhulme's ambitious plan to turn a sleepy crofting township into a major fishing port, see page 72. A tiny, unremarkable village where some of the original buildings can still be seen, this is also the base of the excellent **Am Bothan Bunkhouse** (see Sleeping, page 78) and the departure point for CalMac's car ferry to Berneray. ►► *For further details, see Transport page 80.*

Ròghadal (Rodel)

Three miles east of Leverburgh, at the southeastern tip of Harris, is Ròghadal (Rodel), dominated by the beautiful 12th-century **St Clement's Church**, something of an unusual sight in such a remote spot and one of the most impressive religious building in the Hebrides. (Only the Benedictine abbey on Iona is larger.) The church stands on a site that dates back 1500 years and was built by Alastair Crotach (Hunchback) Macleod of Harris in the 1520s. Though impressive from the outside, particularly the huge tower, the real interest lies in the silent, chilly atmosphere of the interior, where you'll find a collection of remarkable carved wall tombs, some blackened by fire that once ravaged these walls. There are three tombs, the most notable of which is that of the founder, Alastair Crotach. The one in the south wall of the choir is also worth a close look.

Na Baigh (Bays)

Running north from Ròghadal up the east coast of South Harris is the **Golden Road**, so named by the locals because the of the huge cost of building it. This twisting, tortuous single-track road runs through a bizarre and striking moonscape, and driving through it is a unique experience (but keep your eyes on the road or you'll end up in one of the many narrow sea lochs). It seems inconceivable that anyone could survive in such an environment, but the road passes through a string of townships, including picturesque **Geocrab**, all created in the 19th century by the people evicted from the west coast. People here have spent years eking a meagre living from the thin soil by building 'lazy beds' (thin strips of piled-up earth between the rocks) for planting potatoes. Weaving and fishing also provide much-needed income.

At **Lingreabhagh (Lingarabay)** the road skirts the foot of **Roinebhal**, which was, until recently, the proposed site of one of the largest super-quarries in Europe. This would have demolished virtually the entire mountain over many decades. Local people and environmentalists fought a successful campaign to prevent the proposal going ahead, thus protecting a precious natural asset (see box, above). Today, it's not quarries but wind farm developments that threaten to blight the landscape of the Outer Hebrides. The road passes through a succession of tiny settlements before joining the A859 just south of Tarbert.

Na Hearadh (Harris) listings

For Sleeping and Eating price codes and other relevant information, see pages 12-18.

Sleeping

North Harris *p73*

£££ Ardhasaig House, Aird Asaig, 4 miles northwest of Tarbert off A859, T01859-50200, www.ardhasaig.co.uk. Open all year. 6 en suite rooms. Small hotel with a big reputation, especially for its wonderful cooking (4-course set dinner is £40 a head). Lovely location, good disabled facilities and also offers romantics accommodation in a cosy, self-contained barn. Self-catering available from £300 per week.

£ Gatliff Trust Youth Hostel, Rhenigidale, www.gatliff.org.uk. Spectacular location at the head of remote Loch Seaforth. Here you'll find a converted croft house (no phone), which sleeps 13 and is open all year. If properly equipped you can walk the 5 miles from Tarbert using the path once trod by the schoolchildren.

Tarbert and around *p74*

Harris isn't lacking in places to stay, most notably there are luxurious self-catering accommodation and comfortable hotels or guesthouses. Some hotels may offer a room-only rate if you are catching the 0730 ferry back to Skye on Mon, Wed and Fri.

£££ Ceol na Mara, at Direcleit, just mins drive from Tarbert, T01859-502464. Stands above a sea loch and offers 4 comfortable rooms and the option of a 3-course Hebridean dinner (♥♥♥). The Gaelic name translates as 'Music of the Sea.'

£££ Harris Hotel, on the main road from Stornoway, on the left, before the turning for the ferry, Tarbert, T01859-502154. Built in 1865 and sporting the initials of the acclaimed 19th century novelist J M Barrie in its window, this welcoming hotel has 22 comfortable bedrooms to retire to after enjoying a fine meal or malt in the bar.

£££ Hotel Hebrides, beside the ferry pier, Tarbert, T01859-502364, www.hotel-hebrides. com. Extensively refurbished in 2008, this boutique-style 21-room hotel includes luxurious family and double rooms. From the revamped **Pierhouse Restaurant** you can enjoy views over the sea whilst tucking into breakfast or a dinner of fresh seafood (♥♥♥-♥♥).

££ Avalon Guesthouse, 12 West Side, Tarbert, just under a mile before Tarbert on left-hand side of road coming from Stornoway, T01859-502 334, www.avalon guesthouse.org. Open all year. 3 rooms. Comfortable B&B on family croft, wonderful views over Loch West Tarbert.

££ Hirta House, Scalpay, T01859-540394, www.hirtahouse.com. Open all year. 3 lovely en suite rooms. Great sea views and a guest lounge and library. Good value.

££ Mrs C MacKinnon, Highcroft, Ardnakillie, Scalpay, T01859-540305 www.harriscroft. com. Open year-round. 3 rooms in a modern crofthouse. 5 miles from Tarbert with views to East Loch Tarbert and the surrounding hills.

££ Mrs Flora Morrison, Tigh na Mara, Tarbert, T01859-502270 www.tigh-na-mara. co.uk. A B&B within 5 mins' walk of the ferry pier, very friendly.

South Harris p75

££££-£££ Scarista House, Scaristabeg, T01859- 550238, www.scaristahouse.com. Open all year. 5 tastefully furnished rooms and 2 comfortable self-catering cottages at the rear of this 19th century former manse. The bedrooms are well equipped in a residence that truly oozes old world character. Antiques and books greet guests, who can then relax by the roaring open fire with a malt or bottle of fine wine (there's an extensive collection). Forget the TV. This is where to enjoy fantastic company, and an evening meal (£42 for 3 courses and £50 for 4) and even impromptu live ceilidh music. Recommended.

£££ Grimsdale, Leverburgh, T01859-520460, www.grimsdale.co.uk. Run by Effie MacLeod is a friendly, 3-bedroom family guesthouse with wonderful views.

£££ Rodel Hotel, Rodel, T01859-520210, www.rodelhotel.co.uk. Closed Jan to mid-Feb. 4 en suite rooms. Overlooking a tiny harbour at the southern tip of the island and close to St Clement's Church. Comfortable, with a reasonable restaurant (¶¶).

££ Beul Na Mara, Seilebost, T01859-550205, www.buelnamara.co.uk. A 3-bedroom guesthouse on the west coast between Tarbert and Leverburgh, that enjoys the backdrop, golden beaches and of Taransay off-shore. Also offers dinner (¶¶¶ (£25 per person)).

££ Carminish House, 10 mins' walk from the Leverburgh ferry, T01859-520400, www.carminish.com. Offers views over the sea. Dinner is offered (£21) (**££**).

££ Mrs Paula Williams, Sorrel Cottage, 2 Glen, Leverburgh, T01859-520319,

www.sorrelcottage.co.uk. Open all year. 3 rooms. Relaxing place to stay, with meals available, including vegetarian (**££** with dinner, **£** for room only), and cycle hire.

£ Am Bothan Bunkhouse, Leverburgh, T01859-520251, www.ambothan.com. Open all year. A fabulous, well equipped and friendly bunkhouse packed with character and situated close to the pier. Space for tents.

£ Drinishader Bunkhouse, Drinishader, 3 miles south of Tarbert, Bays, T01859-511255. Open all year. 12 beds. Traditional crofters cottage by the sea, with a cosy coal fire. Easily accessed by bus from Tarbert, and there's a shop close by but the nearest pub is 4 miles away.

Self-catering

Blue Reef Cottages, overlooking Scarista beach, T01859-550370, www.stay-hebrides. com. Couples who seek the ultimate in luxurious self-catering need look no further than here. Fashioned from local stone and timbers, these identical 2 croft cottages built into the hillside enjoy breathtaking views over the machair (and golf course) to the Atlantic and offshore Isle of Taransay. There's champagne and home-baking on arrival, bikes and golf clubs to use, a fabulous kitchen, comfy sofas, a wood burning stove and after a day hillwalking or at sea, a jacuzzi and sauna to enjoy before retiring into the tastefully furnished bedroom with its hints of Harris tweed and Queen-sized bed. You'll never want to leave. From £950 per week. Recommended.

Croft Cottage, 5 mins walk from Tarbert T01859-502338, www.croftcottageharris. co.uk. A wonderfully luxurious self-catering option. Ingeniously converted from a former byre and with stunning views over East Loch Tarbert towards the Minch. 3-bedroom, family-friendly hideaway packed with stylish finishes, including solid oak floors and an irresistible sauna and jacuzzi. From £500 (3 days) or from £945 per week. Recommended.

Camping
In Luskentyre, you can **camp** on the machair, but ask for permission at the 1st house.

🍴 Eating

Harris may be small and remote but the enterprising islanders can guarantee that even in the depths of winter you can enjoy a snack, lunch or full-blown candlelit dinner in style. However, it's advisable to book ahead just to ensure the restaurant/café is open. For more information on Harris in winter, see www.winterharris.com.

Tarbert and around p74
♦♦♦-♦♦ Harris Hotel, see Sleeping, above. Serves tasty food every day till around 2100. They do a 3-course fixed menu and reasonably priced bar meals.
♦ First Fruits Tearoom, Tarbert, T01859-502439. Easter-end Aug Mon-Sat 1030-1700. Cosy traditional Hebridean tea room serving delicious home-baking.

Self-catering
♦♦♦-♦♦ Atlantic Edge, T01859-520766, T077866-85156. It's the self-caterers dream with the home-delivery of delicious, gourmet, home-cooked starters (from £3.50), mains (from £12) and desserts (£5.50) right to your door. Feast on the likes of smoked fish pâté with oatcakes, or lemon and ginger soup followed by local lamb with apricots and chocolate roulade.

South Harris p75
♦♦♦-♦♦ Scarista House, Scaristabeg, T01859-550238, www.scaristahouse.com. For a mouth-watering 4-course dinner that may include local lamb, freshly caught shellfish and heavenly desserts, followed by a malt or glass of wine by the fire, you'll not beat the culinary experience at this homely former Georgian manse with views towards the sea. Book ahead. Fabulous and recommended.
♦♦-♦ The Anchorage, by the pier, Leverburgh, T01859-520225. Open Mar-Sep. Café/restaurant near the bunkhouse, offering reasonable lunches and dinners including seafood.
♦♦-♦ Skoon Art Café, Geocrab, T01859-530268, www.skoon.com. Open all year. Overlooking the rocky Bays area on the east coast, this cosy, bright traditional croft house is adorned with the artworks of the resident artist-cum-chef, Andy. His wife, Emma, serves up the delicious soups, sandwiches and home-baking. Recommended.

🎣 Activities and tours

Tarbert and aroun,d p74
Fishing
Obbe Fishings, Leverburgh T01859-520466, www.obbefishings.com. Will help you hook the freshest supper.

Tour operators
Angus Mackay, T01859-550260, www.visit-taransay.com. The man to call for a boat trip to the tiny Isle of Taransay. Leaves from Horgabost Beach and costs £20, children £10.
Bill Lawson, Leverburgh, T01859-520488, www.billlawson.com and **Mike Brigg**, T01859-502376, www.mikeandpeggybriggs.co.uk, offer informative walking trips to spot wildlife.
Hamish Taylor, T01859-530310, www.scenic-cruises.co.uk. Provides wonderful offshore wildlife cruises on the east coast.
Sea Harris, East Tarbert, T01859-502007, www.seaharris.co.uk. Skipper Seumas Morrison offers wildlife and sea trips to the Shiants and St Kilda.

Watersports
For watersports, contact **Adventure Hebrides**, www.adventurehebrides.com; and **Lewis Surf Trek**, T07939-194880, www.lewissurf trek.com. Both based on Lewis.

Harris *p72*

Bus There's a regular bus service between **Tarbert** and **Stornoway**, Mon-Sat, 1 hr 15 mins.

There's a also bus service from **Tarbert** to **Leverburgh** via the east coast (for the ferry to North Uist), 3-4 times daily, 1 hr 5 mins, along the so-called 'Golden Road' and 'Bays' route. This bus service (W13) includes stops at **Drinishader**, **Geocrab** and **Rodel**. To **Huisinis**, 2-4 daily on school days, 45 mins; to **Reinigeadal**, 2 daily on school days; to **Scalpaigh**, 2-5 daily, 10 mins. Bus timetables are available at the TIC or see www.cne-siar.gov.uk.

Cycle hire **Harris Cycle Hire**, Sorrel Cottage, 2 Glen Kyles, Leverburgh, T01859-520319, www.sorrelcottage.co.uk. Prices for bikes start from about £15 per day. Also rents children's bikes.

Ferry A ferry sails from **Leverburgh** to **Berneray**, 3-4 times daily. The trip takes 1 hr and a one-way ticket costs £6.50 per passenger, £29.50 per car (£11.10 and £51 for 5-day saver return). Note that though this is a short crossing, the service can easily be disrupted by high winds so try and be flexible with your travel plans.

The Uists, Benbecula and Barra

South from Harris lies the southern 'half' of the Outer Herbides. The Uists, north and south, and Benbecula are all connected by a series of causeways; you can drive their length, past a never- ending series of fish-filled lochs, windswept beaches backing onto wildflower rich machair and tiny, straggling crofting communities. The quality of the seafood, livestock (and baking) on the Uists also sees these islands make a notable contribution to the acclaimed Outer Hebrides Speciality Food Trail, www.foodhebrides.com. At South Uist's southernmost tip, you cross a half-mile long causeway to the tiny and beautiful Isle of Eriskay where within sight of the beach where Bonnie Prince Charlie first stepped ashore on Scotland in his bid to seize the Scottish Crown for the Stuart's, the road runs out at the CalMac ferry slipway for Barra. Alternatively, you can fly from Glasgow to Barra and land on its famous famous cockle strand – at low tide, of course! ▸ *For listings, see pages 90-94.*

Ins and outs

Getting around

In recent years, the network of public transport on the islands has improved. Nonetheless, if relying on a bus to get around, don't expect one every five minutes – or hour. It is highly recommended to get hold of a free copy of Uist and *Barra, Bus and Ferry services* from TIC's or view the timetables online at www.cne-siar.gov.uk. There are six to seven buses per day (except Sunday) from Berneray to Lochmaddy. Some of these buses continue to Baile a Mhanaich (Balivanich) on Benbecula, where there is an airport, see page 84, and Lochboisdale and Ludag on South Uist, see page 86. There are six to seven buses per day from Lochmaddy to the island of Bearnaraigh (Berneray) just off the north coast in the sound of Harris. There are three buses per day from Lochmaddy to Clachan na Luib (Clachan-a-Luib) which run in an anti-clockwise direction around the north and west coasts. Two buses per day connect Clachan-a-Luib with Baile Sear (Baleshare) and also with Saighdinis (Sidinish).

A mile long causeway connects South Uist to Benbecula by road and regular buses (four per day Monday to Saturday) run between Lochboisdale and Lochmaddy on North Uist, stopping en route at Dalabrog (Daliburgh), Tobha Mòr (Howmore) and Lionacleit and Balinavich on Benbecula. There is also a regular bus service between Lochboisdale and Ludag (for ferries to Barra). A causeway links Eriskay to South Uist. CalMac operates a ferry to Eriskay from Barra, see page 94.

Uibhist a Tuath (North Uist)

→ *For listings, see pages 90-94. Phone code 01876. Population 1815.*

North Uist is the largest island in the southern chain of the Outer Hebrides, about 13 miles from north to south and 18 miles east to west at its widest point. At first sight it comes as something of a disappointment after the dramatic landscapes of Harris. In fact, it's barely a landscape at all, as over a third of the island's surface is covered by water. The east coast around Lochmaddy, the main settlement, is so peppered with lochs it resembles a giant sieve. But, heading west from Lochmaddy, the island's attractions become apparent, particularly the magnificent beaches on the north and west coasts. Also on the west coast, is the Balranald Nature Reserve, the ideal place for birdwatching. You're also likely to see otters. There are numerous prehistoric sites scattered across the island and, with all that water around, there's obviously plenty of good fishing to be had.

Ins and outs

Getting there There are two car ferry services to North Uist. One is to the northern Isle of Berneray (joined to Uist by a causeway) from Leverburgh on South Harris, the other to Lochmaddy from Uig on Skye (one or two daily, the journey takes one hour and 40 minutes), a one-way ticket is £5.35 per person, £24.20 per car. Contact **CalMac** ① *T01876-500337*, in Lochmaddy, for further information. North Uist is joined to the islands of Benbecula and South Uist to the south by a causeway and bridge. There are several buses daily (Monday to Saturday) from Otternish to Lochmaddy and on to Lochboisdale on South Uist.

Loch nam Madadh (Lochmaddy)

Lochmaddy, the island's main village and ferry port, is a tiny place; so small you're almost through it before you realize. Though it's on the east coast and not close to the beaches, it's a good start point (and if devoid of camping equipment) base for exploring the island as it boasts most facilities. It has a bank (next to the tourist office), a hotel and pub, a tourist office, a few shops, post office, hospital, petrol station and the well run **Uist Outdoor Centre** ① *T01876-500480, www.uistoutdoorcentre.co.uk*, where you can enjoy a range of watersports, notably sea kayaking, and stay at its bunkhouse (see Activities and tours, page 93).

If you have time, the **Taigh Chearsabhagh Museum and Arts Centre** ① *T/F01876-500293, www.taigh-chearsabhagh.org, Mon-Sat 1000-1700, free,* is worth visiting and has a small café. You can also purchase home-made preserves, crafts and even Harris tweed handbags. The **TIC** ① *near the ferry pier, T01876-500321, Apr-Oct Mon-Sat 0900-1700, and for the arrival of the evening ferry*, will provide transport timetables and sells a number of useful walking maps if you plan to hike the beaches and hills.

Around the island

There are a number of interesting archaeological sites of different periods dotted around the island. The most notable is **Barpa Langass**, 7 miles southwest of Lochmaddy on the slope of Ben Langass, just off the A867, which cuts across the bleak peaty hinterland of North Uist. This is a huge chambered burial cairn dating from around 3000 BC. Unfortunately, it is now too dangerous to enter. About a mile away, on the southern side of Ben Langass, is the small stone circle known as **Pobull Fhinn**, standing on the edge of Loch Langass. Three miles northwest of Lochmaddy on the A865 are three Bronze Age standing stones called **Na Fir Bhreige** (The False Men), said to be the graves of three spies who were buried alive.

The real charms of North Uist, though, are the fabulous beaches on its north and west coasts. Heading anti-clockwise from Lochmaddy, the A865 runs northwest, passing the turning for Otternish and the wild and beautiful lands of Bearnaraigh (see below), which is now connected to North Uist by a causeway. It continues west through the township of **Sollas (Solas)**, where there are a couple of B&Bs, and then passes the beautiful sands of **Bhalaigh (Vallay) Strand**. Near the northwestern tip of the island, standing on an islet in Loch Scolpaig, is **Scolpaig Tower**, a 'folly' built to provide employment and income for local men in the 19th century.

Three miles south of here is the turning to **Balranald RSPB Reserve**, an area of rocky coast, sandy beaches and dunes, machair and lochs. The reserve is ideal for birdwatching, especially waders. A two-hour guided walk along the headland allows you to see Manx shearwaters, gannets, skuas and storm petrels, and, during the summer, you can listen out for the distinctive rasping call of the corncrake, one of the rarest birds in Britain. There's a basic visitor centre which is open from April to September.

As the road continues south, pop into the sparse but tasty **Claddach Kirkibost Centre and Café** ① *Mon-Sat 1000-1600*, a community enterprise that sells peat smoked salmon, jams and an amazing selection of home-baking, including their famous tablet. A mile further south the A865 meets the A867, which heads east back to Lochmaddy. Staying on the A865, after another mile you can turn off for the tidal and sparsely inhabited island of **Baile Sear (Baleshare)**, now connected by a causeway to North Uist and with a three-mile- long beach from where you can just see the low lying **Monach Isles** (also known by their old Norse name of *Heisker*) lying 5 miles off the west coast. They were once connected to North Uist at low tide until the 16th century, when a huge tidal wave swept away the sand bridge, thus isolating them. Even so, the islands were inhabited until as recently as the 1930s. Now they are populated by the largest breeding colony of grey seals in Europe.

South of Clachan, where a **viewing gallery** ① *Mon-Sat*, provides an insight into the fish smoking process of the acclaimed **Hebridean Smokehouse** ① *T01876-580209, www. hebrideansmokehouse.com*, the road runs past **Cairinis (Carinish)** and the **Carinish Inn** over a series of causeways to the little-visited lobster-fishing island of **Griomasaigh (Grimsay)**, before heading across another causeway to Benbecula. Near Cairinis is **Feith na Fala (Field of Blood)**, site of the last battle fought in Scotland solely with swords and bows and arrows, in 1601, between the MacDonalds of Sleat and Macleods of Harris. The bloodshed was provoked by one of the MacDonalds divorcing his Macleod wife. When 60 Skye Macleods set off to North Uist to wreak revenge, they were met by 16 MacDonalds who literally chopped them to pieces, proving that divorce was a messy business even back then.

Bearnaraigh (Berneray) → *For listings, see pages 90-94. Phone code 01876.*

Ferries from Leverburgh on Harris arrive at the low-lying island of Bearnaraigh (believed to be Old Norse for Bear Island) now connected by a causeway to North Uist. The island, rich in birdlife, is famous as the place where Prince Charles spent a holiday helping out on a croft. It's also the birthplace of Angus 'Giant' MacAskill, see page 313. Its real attraction, though, apart from the splendid isolation and its cosy **Lobster Pot Café** (see Eating, page 92) at Ardmaree is the three-mile-long sandy beach along its western shoreline. On the east coast, there's more stunning white sands, behind which stands the fabulously earthy bunkhouse of the Gatliff Trust with views over the skerries and to the brooding rounded hills of Harris. A ½-mile east of the Lobster Pot is the **Berneray Historical Society and Visitor Centre** ① *Mon-Fri 1100-1500, £1, internet access*, with photographs and exhibits highlighting the hardy life islanders once lived.

A booklet for Bearnaraigh, *Visit Berneray* is available from Lochmaddy TIC. It describes all of the key places of interest, including the 16th-century gunnery at **Baile**, the beaches and machair of the north and west coasts, and archaeological sites dating from the Viking period near **Borgh**. It also highlights a lovely 7½-mile-long circular walk. **Berneray Week** (late July) is a busy week with several ceilidhs held in the community hall and attracting visitors from far afield – including Gaelic speaking Germans!

Beinn na Faoghla (Benbecula)

→ *For listings, see pages 90-94. Phone code 01870. Population 1803.*

Tiny Benbecula may be suffering from delusions of stature. Its Gaelic name means 'mountain of the fords', but the highest point is a mere 407 ft, with the rest of the island as flat as a pancake. It lies between Protestant North Uist and Catholic South Uist, and most visitors use it solely as a means of getting from one to the other via the A865, which cuts straight through the middle.

Ins and outs

Getting there and around Benbecula's airport is at Balivanich and there are direct flights from Glasgow, Barra and Stornoway. **Flybe/Loganair** ① *T0871-700 2000, www.flybe.com*, flies from Glasgow to Benbecula, Monday to Saturday, twice a day and the flight takes one hour. The island is connected by causeways to North and South Uist, and buses travelling from Lochmaddy and Lochboisdale pass through the villages of Balivanich, Lionacleit (Liniclate) and Creag Ghoraidh (Creagorry). There are also regular island buses which run between these settlements. ►► *For further details, see Transport, page 94.*

Sights

Like North Uist, the east of the island is so pitted with lochs that most people live on the west coast. Until recently, a large percentage of the population were Royal Artillery personnel stationed at **Baile a Mhanaich (Balivanich)**, a sprawling, army base of utilitarian buildings in the northwest of the island. There's little to hold your interest in this village dominated by the (albeit diminishing presence) of the military and civilian airport. There is a Bank of Scotland (ATM), a post office and you can browse for high quality tweeds, hand-knitted jumpers, confectionery, prints and jewellery at **MacGillivrays** ① *T01870-602525*, or visit the notable **The Stepping Stone** restaurant.

South of Balivanich, the B892 runs around the west coast offering the opportunity to stroll down miles of white sands before joining the main A865 at the southern end of the island. It runs past **Culla Bay**, overlooked by **Baille nan Cailleach (Nunton)**. It was from here in 1746 that Bonnie Prince Charlie set off with Flora MacDonald over the sea to Skye, disguised as her maid, see box, page 311. To the south is **Poll-na-Crann**, better known as 'stinky bay' because of the piles of seaweed deposited there by fierce Atlantic storms. From the mid-18th century this kelp was used to provide soda ash for making glass, and provided a source of income for many communities. By 1820 the so-called kelp boom was over, but it is still gathered today and used for fertilizer.

The B892 ends at **Lionacleit (Liniclate)**, where the community school serves the Uists and Benbecula. It has extensive facilities, including internet, a swimming pool, library, theatre and even a small local history **museum** ① *Mon, Tue and Thu 0900-1600, Wed 0900-1230, 1330-1600, Fri 0900-2000, Sat 1100-1300, 1400-1600, free.* Close by, there's a very large Co-op supermarket, the only one for miles around.

Tight little island

Between Eriskay and South Uist is the wreck of the famous SS Politician, the island's other claim to fame. In 1941 the 12,000 ton ship went aground just off the island of Calvey and sank with its cargo, which included 20,000 cases of whisky. This not only provided many islanders with a supply of whisky for many years, but also provided the plot for Compton Mackenzie's book *Whisky Galore!*, which was later made into the famous Ealing comedy of the same name (called Tight Little Island in the US) and filmed on Barra. It's very difficult to spot the wreck, even at low tide, but if you pop into the friendly Am Politician pub in the village on Eriksay, Baile (Balla), you'll find more information and some memorabilia.

Uibhist a Deas (South Uist)

→ *For listings, see pages 90-94. Phone code 01870. Population 2285.*

South Uist is the largest of the southern chain of Outer Hebridean islands and like North Uist and Berneray isn't lacking in wildlife, fishing and dramatic scenery. However, like its southern neighbour, Barra, South Uist is Roman Catholic and generally more relaxed about Sunday openings. Its 20 miles of west coast is one long sandy beach, backed by dunes with a mile or two of beautiful, flowering machair behind. To the east of the main A865 which runs the length of the island, rises a central mountainous spine of rock and peat dotted with numerous lochs. Its two highest peaks, **Beinn Mhor** (2034 ft) and **Hecla** (1988 ft), tower over the rocky cliffs of an inaccessible eastern coastline indented by sea lochs.

Ins and outs

Getting there The island's main ferry port is Lochboisdale, which is reached from Oban four times a week (arriving at night) and twice a week from Castlebay on Barra. There's one direct sailing from Oban on Tuesday, Thursday and Saturday (five hours and 20 minutes), and one via Castlebay (Barra) on Sunday (six hours and 30 minutes). There are also early morning departures (0700) from Castlebay on Wednesday and Friday, and at 2010 on Sundays. A Oban to Lochboisdale one-way ticket is £11.80 per passenger, £53 per car. A private passenger-only ferry sails from Barra to Ludag, at the southern tip of South Uist, on Sunday. There are limited bus services on Sundays. ►► *For further details, see Transport page 94.*

Background

The dominant family in South Uist was Clanranald, who also owned Benbecula. They were descendants of the first Lord of the Isles, who was a MacDonald. The island's connections with Clanranald came to a sorry end, however, in 1837, when it was sold, along with Benbecula, to pay off bad debts, and became the property of the infamous Lieutenant-Colonel John Gordon of Cluny. Though all the southern isles suffered during the brutal Clearances of the 19th century, the experiences of people on South Uist were particularly cruel and inhumane. Between 1849 and 1851 over 2000 were forcibly shipped to Quebec in Canada. Those who refused to board the transport ships were hunted down by dogs and bound, before being thrown on board and shipped to Canada, where they were left to starve. Today, owned by the community, the destiny of South Uist fortunately lies in the islanders' hands.

Loch Baghasdail (Lochboisdale) → *Phone code 01878.*

South Uist's largest settlement is set on a rocky promontory in a beautiful island-dotted sea loch. The imposing entrance is guarded by Calvay Island with its 13th-century castle ruin. Lochboisdale is a tiny place, with little in the way of tourist sights, though it does have a hotel, bank, post office and TIC ① *Pier Rd, T01878-700286, early Apr to mid-Oct.*

About 10 miles south of Lochboisdale, on the southern coast of the island, is **Ludag jetty**, the departure point for the small private passenger ferry to **Eòlaigearraidh (Eoligarry)** on (45 minutes) Barra T01851-701702. At **Cille Bhrìghde (West Kilbride)** nearby is **Hebridean Croft Originals** ① *open daily*, which has a wide range of local crafts on show, as well as a photographic display of local history and a tea room.

Around the island

At the north of the island a causeway leads across **Loch Bi** (pronounced 'Bee') to the distinctive modern statue of Our Lady of the Isles, standing by the main road on the lower slopes of **Rueval Hill**. Further up the hill is the Royal Artillery control centre, known by the locals as 'Space City', due to its forest of aerials and 'golf balls', which tracks the missiles fired from a range on the northwestern corner of the island out into the Atlantic. However, to home in on delicious food and a comfortable stay, it's worthwhile following the signs for the **Orasay Inn** ① *T01870-610298, www.orasayinn.com*, by Lochcarnan and where just 1½ miles further down the road, you can further tickle your tastebuds by popping into the shop of the acclaimed **Salar Smokehouse** ① *www.salar.co.uk.*

Just to the south of here is **Loch Druidibeag Nature Reserve**, on the site of the large freshwater loch, one of the largest breeding grounds in the British Isles for greylag geese and also a favourite haunt of mute swans (there's a warden nearby at Groigearraidh Lodge). From here the main road runs down the spine of the island; all along the way little tracks branch off to the west, leading down to lovely beaches.

Not far south of Loch Druidibeag is the turning to the tiny village of **Tobha Mòr (Howmore)**, where you can see a collection of old traditional thatched blackhouses beside the seemingly endless stretch of golden sand. One of the houses has been converted into a **Gatliff Trust Youth Hostel**, see Sleeping, page 98. From the hostel, it's a five-minute walk across the machair to the sandy beach which stretches almost the entire length of South Uist.

Periodically, down the A865 you'll spot signs for accessing paths across the machair. In addition, from Tobha Mòr, there are superb walks through the lonely hills of **Beinn Mhor** (620 m), **Beinn Corodale** (527 m) and **Hecla** (606 m) to the picturesque and dramatic valleys of Glen Hellisdale, Glen Corodale and Glen Usinish on the east coast. In 1746 that ubiquitous troglodyte, Bonnie Prince Charlie is reputed to have taken refuge in a cave above **Corodale Bay** for three weeks after his defeat and escape from Culloden.

Near **Bornais (Bornish)** another minor road can be followed east of the A865 to **Loch Eynort**, which penetrates far inland from the Minch. An old stalkers' path can be followed along the north shore of the loch towards the sea, with views of numerous seals, the occasional otter and the steep upper slopes of Beinn Mhor towering above to the north.

A few miles south, at **Gearraidh Bhailteas (Milton)**, a memorial cairn sits amidst the ruins of the cottage that was Flora (Flory) MacDonald's birthplace, that famous Hebridean lass who helped save the skin of Bonnie Prince Charlie, see box, page 311. Nearby is the **Kildonan Museum** ① *Apr-Oct Mon-Sat 1000-1700, Sun 1400-1700*, with exhibits of the area's history, craft work and archaeology. There's also a tea room. A few miles further on, the A865 cuts east to the island's main ferry port of **Lochboisdale**. For those in search of great food and tremendous views towards Eriskay and Barra, leave the A865 for the B888 and enjoy the hospitality of the 17th century **Polochar Inn** (see Sleeping, page 98) on the southwestern tip of South Uist.

Eirisgeidh (Eriskay) → *For listings, see pages 90-94. Phone code 01878.*

The tiny island of Eriskay, with a population of less than 200, gives its name to the native breed of pony, said to have been ridden by King Robert the Bruce at the Battle of Bannockburn in 1314. In the late 1970s the ponies nearly became extinct, but one surviving stallion saved the breed and numbers are growing. A series of paths take you around the island in about three hours. For more details, see the *Cuairt Eirisgeidh* leaflet published by Visit Hebrides and available at the Lochboisdale TIC.

Most people come to Eriskay to pay a visit to **Coilleag a' Phrionnsa (Prince's beach)**, the sandy beach on the west coast and just 220 yds from the CalMac jetty that will take you to neighbouring Barra. The beach is where Bonnie Prince Charlie first stepped on to Scottish soil on 23 July 1745, at the start of the ill-fated Jacobite Rebellion. The rare pink convolvulus (field bindweed) which grows there today is said to have been planted by the Prince himself from seeds brought from France. A small memorial cairn in the dunes behind the beach was erected by the local school to commemorate the occasion.

It's now almost impossible to see the wreck of the *SS Politician* (see box, page 85) when crossing the causeway from South Uist (look left), but at the **Am Politician** pub you can (carefully) hold an original whisky bottle taken from its hold and look at other artefacts from the wreck. Another sight worth seeing is **St Michael's**, the Roman Catholic church built in 1903 and funded by the local fishing fleet.

Bharraigh (Barra) → *For listings, see pages 90-94. Phone code 01871. Population 1316.*

It may be tempting to overlook the little island of Barra, only about 8 miles long by 5 miles wide, but that would be a mistake, as it's one of the most beautiful of all the islands in the Outer Hebrides – 'Barradise' indeed. Here, despite an appalling lack of public toilets (there's only three: at the Ardmhor Ferry Terminal, Eoligarry and Castlebay Hall) and much needed facilities for campers (wild camping is tolerated) you'll find the best of the islands in miniature – beaches, machair, peat-covered hills, tiny crofting communities and Neolithic remains. A couple of days spent on Barra, including excursions to the wild and beautiful lands of Vatersay and the outlying (deserted) Isle of Mingulay, gives a real taste of Hebridean life. Gaelic and the traditional fishing culture is also strong here but, with its Catholicism, Barra is arguably more laid-back than its northern neighbours which strictly observe the Sabbath.

Ins and outs
Getting there The best way to arrive is by air at Tràigh Mhòr ('Cockle Strand'), the famous airstrip on the beach at the north end of the island. This is the only airport in the UK where flight schedules are shown as 'subject to tides' and wild campers are warned to keep off the beach on hearing the drone of an aircraft! **Flybe/Loganair** ① *T0871-700 2000, www. flybe.com*, flies from Glasgow to Barra, Monday to Saturday once a day. The journey takes one hour and five minutes.

Barra is most easily reached by car ferry from Oban on the mainland, by car ferry from Lochboisdale on South Uist (Monday at 0730, Tuesday at 1900 and Thursday at 2100,

Net profit

Rather than watch their island be destroyed by the elements, the redoubtable inhabitants of tiny Vatersay have taken matters into their own hands. The northern and southern ends of the island are linked by a narrow, 600-yd-long isthmus and, in recent years, raging Atlantic storms have washed away parts of it. Fearing that their island might be split in two, crofters have fixed some old salmon nets from fish farms onto the beach, secured with wires and old wooden pallets, to prevent the sand being scattered by the gales. Over time, the build up of sand trapped in the netting can link up with the machair, thus allowing grass and flowers to grow. Hopefully, over time, successive layers of sand and earth will be built up to protect the coastline. About 100 yds of beach have so far been protected using this rudimentary method, and the island's local authority is donating £3000 so that the whole 600-yd stretch linking the two ends of Vatersay can be saved. News of the crofters' ingenuity and resourcefulness has spread and the plan is being adopted on nearby Barra, where erosion is also a serious problem.

one hour 40 minutes, £7 one-way per passenger, £20.30 per car) and from Eriskay, or by a private passenger-only **ferry** ① *T01878-720238*, that sails from Ludag on South Uist to Eoligarry. There is one direct sailing a day from Oban, except Tuesday and Thursday. The journey takes four hours and 50 minutes. The sailing from Oban to Castlebay via Lochboisdale is on Tuesday and Thursday (seven hours and 20 minutes) and one-way costs £11.80 per passenger and £53 per car.

Getting around There is a regular bus/postbus service (Monday to Saturday) that runs from Castlebay to the ferry port of Eòlaigearraidh, via the airport. There are also buses (Monday-Saturday) from Castlebay to Bhatarsaigh (Vatersay). You can hire a car or a bicycle to tour the island at your leisure. It's 14 miles round the main road. ▶▶ *For further details, see Transport page 94.*

Bàgh a' Chaisteil (Castlebay)

The main settlement is Castlebay, on the southern side of the island, situated in a wide sheltered bay and overlooked by **Sheabhal** (383 m), on top of which is a marble statue of the Blessed Virgin and Child. It's a short but steep walk up to the top from the town, and the views are well worth it. The once-thriving herring port is also overlooked by the large Roman Catholic church, **Our Lady, Star of the Sea**.

As the main ferry port, rather drab Castlebay provides the full range of services: hotels, B&Bs, shops, petrol, a bank (with ATM) and post office. The **TIC** ① *T01871-810336, Apr to mid-Oct Mon-Sat 0900-1700, Sun 1200-1600 and also open for the arrival of the evening ferry*, is on the main street near the ferry terminal. It sells handy leaflets on local walks (50p) including Vatersay, tickets for the castle (below) and will book accommodation.

Castlebay's most notable feature is the impressive 15th-century **Kisimul Castle** ① *T01871-810313, Apr-Sep daily 0930-1230, 1330-1730, £4.70, concessions £3.80, children £2.80, including boat trip*, reached by boat from Castlebay pier (five minutes), weather permitting, built on an island in the middle of the harbour. This was the ancient home of the Chief of the MacNeils, one of the oldest Scottish clans, who owned the island from 1427 until 1838. It was then sold to the notorious Colonel Gordon of Cluny, along with neighbouring South Uist and Benbecula (see page 85), and the poor people of Barra suffered the same cruel fate, 600 of them being shipped to Canada to starve. One hundred years later the castle and much of the island was bought back for the MacNeils by an American architect, Robert Lister MacNeil, who became the 45th Clan Chief and restored the castle to its present state before his death in 1970. His son, Ian Roderick MacNeil, used it as his residence when visiting the island, before handing it over to Historic Scotland in 2000 on a 1000-year lease, in exchange for a rent of £1 and a bottle of whisky.

If you're interested in finding out about the island's history, you should visit the Barra Heritage Cultural Centre, known as **Dualchas** ⓘ *T01871-810413, May-end Aug Mon-Sat 1030-1630, Mar, Apr and Sep Mon, Wed and Fri, £2, concessions £1.50, children £1.*

Around the island

The A888 follows a circular route of 14 miles around the island, making an ideal day's bike tour from Castlebay. Heading west, it passes the turning for the causeway to **Vatersay** (see below), then runs north past stunning beaches including **Halaman Bay**, near the village of Tangasdal (**Tangasdale**) and overlooked by the Isle of Barra Hotel (see Sleeping, page 98), before climbing between two hills (Sheabhal to the east and Beinn Tangabhal to the west). Before reaching the north coast, at the turning for **Borgh** (**Borve**) there are standing stones followed by the small settlement of **Baile Na Creige** (**Craigston**), where you'll find the **An Dubharaidh Thatched Cottage Museum** ⓘ *Easter-Oct Mon-Fri 1100-1700, £2*, an original whitehouse and the chambered burial cairn of **Dun Bharpa**. From Dun Bharpa there are pleasant walks into the surrounding hills, with the summit of **Sheabhal** offering tremendous views from the highest point on the island.

Near **Allathsdal** (**Allasdale**), is another lovely beach, and just beyond are the remains of **Dun Cuier**, an Iron Age fort. Make a short detour at Grein, and follow the headland to the rugged cliffs at **Grein Head**.

The A888 then descends eastwards to **Bagh a Tuath** (**Northbay**), where a branch left leads to the village of **Eòlaigearraidh** (**Eoligarry**), near the northern tip, surrounded by sandy bays washed by Atlantic rollers. A private passenger ferry leaves from here to Ludag on South Uist.

The road to Eoligarry passes the island's airport at **Tràigh Mhòr**, the 'Cockle Strand', which once provided 100 to 200 cartloads of delicious cockles each day. Now the cockle-shells are gathered and used for harling, the roughcast wall covering used on many Scottish houses. By the beach is the house that was once the home of Compton MacKenzie, author of *Whisky Galore!*, see box, page 85. He lies buried at picturesque **Cille Bhara**, to the west of the village of Eòlaigearraidh, along with members of the MacNeil clan. This was one of the most important religious complexes in the Outer Hebrides, built in the 12th century, and consists of a tiny church and two chapels. One of these, St Mary's, has been re-roofed and houses several carved medieval tombstones and a copy of a runic stone. Much to the chagrin of locals, the original stone is in the Museum of Scotland in Edinburgh.

Bhatarsaigh (Vatersay) and Mingulay → *For listings, see pages 90-94.*

A worthwhile trip from Castlebay is to the island of Vatersay, linked since 1990 to Barra by a causeway built in an effort to stabilize the tiny community (around 70) on what is the most southerly inhabited Outer Hebridean island. Home to the acclaimed folk singing group The Vatersay Boys, it boasts several idyllic sands including two shell-sand beaches backed by machair, only a few hundred yards apart on either side of the narrow isthmus that leads to the main settlement of Vatersay. On the west beach, Bagh Siar, is the **Annie**

Jane Monument, commemorating the terrible tragedy in 1853, when the emigrant ship *Annie Jane* was wrecked off the coast of Vatersay, with the loss of 333 lives, many of them islanders. There's a scenic 4-mile circular walk from the monument and the Barra TIC sells a map of the route. You can buy coffee and sandwiches at the **Vatersay village hall** ① *Apr-Oct 1000-1700*, (also, note, the only public toilets on the island), and wild camp or park your campervan nearby (£4 donation to the Vatersay Township).

On a clear day from Vatersay you can enjoy the view of the smaller islands to the south – Sandray, Pabbay and Mingulay. The latter was inhabited until 1912 and can still be visited from Barra. It was acquired by the National Trust for Scotland in 2000. ▸▸ *For details of tours, see Barra Fishing Charters, page 93.*

The Uists, Benbecula and Barra listings

For Sleeping and Eating price codes and other relevant information, see pages 12-19.

⊖ Sleeping

North Uist *p82*

££££ Tigh Dearg Hotel, Lochmaddy, T01876- 500700, www.tigh-dearg-hotel. co.uk. Open all year. 8 en suite rooms. Stylish and contemporary, from the bright red exterior (the name means 'Red House') to the designer rooms, it offers DVD/CD players,a highly rated restaurant and a leisure club with fully equipped gym, sauna and steam room. By the way, it's pronounced 'tie-jerack'.

£££ Langass Lodge, near Pobhull Fhinn, T01876-580285, www.langasslodge.co.uk. 12 en suite rooms. Stylish and comfortable accommodation in this secluded hotel over-looking a sea loch. Friendly, and welcomes children. The restaurant has a menu rich in local seafood and game (dinner ¶¶¶). Recommended.

£££ Temple View Hotel, on the main road, Carinish, T01876-580676, www.templeview hotel.co.uk. This is a lovely, modest family-run guesthouse with views towards the 13th century ruin of Trinity Temple.

£££-££ Lochmaddy Hotel, right by the ferry terminal, Lochmaddy, T01876-500332, www.lochmaddy hotel.co.uk. Open all year. 15 en suite rooms (8 with sea view). Recently refurnished and fully Wi-Fi accessible. rooms. The restaurant and bar serve good-value food (¶¶-¶) in a pleasant setting. Also offers

takeaway (¶) burgers, fish, etc, daily 1730-2030. This is the place to ask about fishing, as they rent out boats and sell permits for trout and salmon fishing. Proud of its walker- and cycle-friendly status, and this is reflected in its drying rooms and lockable bike storage facilities for guests.

££ Ardnastruban House, just off the A865, Grimsay, T01870-602452, www.ardnastruban house.co.uk. Open Jan-Dec. This friendly guesthouse is surrounded by wildlife and rugged scenery.

££ Bagh Alluin, 21 Baleshare, T01876-580370, www.jacvolbeda.co.uk. Has 3 very spacious, modern bedrooms.

££ Mrs Morag Nicholson, The Old Shop House, Bayhead, T01876-510395. Has 2 en suite rooms and offers friendly and comfortable B&B.

££ Sgeir Ruadh , near Balranald, Houghgarry, T01876-510312, sgeirruadh@aol.com. Run by Mrs Simpson this good value B&B is open all year. It has 3 en suite rooms, overlooks a beautiful beach and is perfect for bird-watchers as it's within the Clanranald Reserve.

Self-catering

Tigh na Boireach, Clachan Sands, T01876-560403. Sleep in a 4-poster bed in 1 of 2 modernized yet traditional thatched croft cottages surrounded by wildlife and rugged scenery. From £350 per week. Sleeps 2.

Uist Outdoor Centre, half a mile from the ferry pier, Lochmaddy, T01876-500234, 500480, www.uistoutdoorcentre.co.uk. Open all year. Independent hostel with room for up to 20 in 4-person bunk rooms (£15 per person per night). Offers a full range of facilities, outdoor activities and courses (see Activities and tours, page 93). Full board is also available. Prices on application.

Berneray *p83*

£ Burnside Croft, near 3 mile west beach, T01876-540235, www.burnsidecroft.com. Here you can share Prince Charles' (not the Bonnie one) crofting experience with Don Alick (Splash) MacKillop and his Australian wife Gloria, who cooks up a storm in the kitchen. Guests can place a stone on the 'mosaic of friendship', a drystone dyke that attests to the welcoming atmosphere here. The hosts also offer fishing and boat trips to uninhabited islands and Don Alick is a storyteller in the great Hebridean tradition for evenings round the fire. Excellent walking, birdlife and beaches in the area. From £680 per week. Sleeps 2.

£ Gatliff Trust Hostel, 1 mile up the east coast from the old ferry pier, www.gatliff. co.uk/berneray.php, T0870-1553255. Open all year, no advance bookings. Affiliated to the SYHA. Relax in 2 restored and truly rustic blackhouses overlooking a lovely sandy beach and old Viking pier. 12 beds, shower, no phone. It's far from luxurious but it's true old-world, earthy hostelling and the views are priceless. £10 for a hostel bed, £5 to camp. Recommended.

Benbecula *p84*

£££ Isle of Benbecula House Hotel, Creag Ghoraidh, T01870-602024, www.isleshotel group.co.uk. Open all year. 20 en suite rooms. Meals served in conservatory dining room (à la carte dinner £30 per person ♥♥♥-♥♥), with sea views.

££ Creag Liath, 1½ miles off the road, Griminish, T01870-602992. Comfortable 2-bedroom option on a working croft.

Camping
Shellbay Caravan and Camping Park, Lionacleit, T01870-602447. Open Apr-Oct. £6 per pitch.

South Uist *p85*

£££ Lochboisdale Hotel, close to the ferry terminal, Lochboisdale, T01878-700332, www.lochboisdalehotel.com. Open all year. 16 en suite rooms. Family-owned hotel with music sessions every fortnight and frequent, spontaneous outbreaks of fiddling by the open fire.

£££ Polochar Inn, a few miles to the west of Ludag, Pollachar, T01878-700215, www.polocharinn.com. Open all year. 11 comfortable en suite rooms. Terrific food (see Eating, below), stunning views towards Barra. A small, refurbished hotel steeped in history, with its 1750 built walls and Neolithic standing stone by the shore. Recommended.

£££-££ Borrodale Hotel, at the junction where the road splits south to Eriskay and east to Lochboisdale, Dalabrog, T01878-700444, www.isleshotelgroup.co.uk. 12 room hotel. Hearty lunch (♥) from 1200 and dinner (♥♥) from 1800-2100.

££ Anglers Retreat, Ardmore, T01870-610325, www.anglersretreat.net. Mar-Dec. 4 en suite rooms. Comfortable, modern guesthouse that's perfect for the keen angler and birdwatcher.

££ Orasay Inn, Lochcarnan, T01878-610298, www.orasayinn.com. Open all year. 9 en suite rooms. Small, friendly, family-run hotel. Reasonable rooms but the restaurant (1200-2100) is the star attraction, serving up delicious lunches (♥) and dinners (♥♥): seafood such as scallops with bacon or freshly caught crab. Recommended.

££-£ Caloraidh, Milton, T01878-710365. Open all year. 2 bedrooms with one suitable for disabled visitors. Friendly, comfortable and handy for the Askernish golf course, Kildonan Museum and Flora MacDonald's birthplace.

£ Gatliff Trust Youth Hostel, Howmore, www.gatliff.co.uk/howmore.php, T0870-155 3255. Open all year. Converted black-house which overlooks the ruins of an ancient church and graveyard, beside the seemingly endless stretch of golden sand. 13 beds, no phone. The warden of the hostel also runs **Rothan Cycles**, see Transport, page 94.

Eriskay p87
Self-catering
Aird na Haun There is a 2-bedroom self-catering flat (T0141-3392143, www.visit eriskay.com), by the beach that can be rented from £300 per week.

Camping
You can wild camp but there are few amenities other than a shop, post office and the pub.

Barra p87
It's a good idea to book in advance if arriving on the evening ferry from Oban. There are neither independent hostels nor a Gatliff Trust Hostel on Barra. Complex crofting laws mean that provision for campers and motorhomes remains woefully inadequate, although one is planned for Borve in Spring 2011.
£££-££ Castlebay Hotel, overlooking the ferry terminal and Kisimul Castle, Castlebay, T01871-810223, www.castlebayhotel.com. Open all year.10 en suite rooms. **££** including dinner (1800-2100). Arguably, the best place to stay on the island, combining comfort with tasty, good value food (♥♥♥-♥♥) and a lively, adjoining public bar.
£££-££ Craigard Hotel, Castlebay, T01871-810200, www.craigardhotel.co.uk. Open all year. 7 en suite rooms. Great views from the conservatory over the bay, reasonable food and walls adorned with photos from the filming of *Whisky Galore!*.
£££-££ Isle of Barra Hotel, 2 miles west of Castlebay, T01871-810383, www.isleofbarra hotel.co.uk 38 en suite rooms, and a good restaurant (♥♥♥-♥♥) and selection of bar food (♥). Fabulous views of the white sands below, though the 1970s exterior isn't exactly in keeping with the landscape. It's only open Apr-Sep.
££ Heathbank Hotel, T01871-890266, www.barrahotel.co.uk. 5 spotless en suite rooms of varying sizes with a pub downstairs.
££-£ Tigh-Na-Mara, Castlebay, T01871-810304, www.tighnamara-barra.co.uk. Open all year. 5 rooms. Comfortable guesthouse only a few mins' walk from the ferry terminal.

£ Dunard Hostel, just along from the Co-op and Heritage Museum, Castlebay, T01871-810443, www.dunardhostel.co.uk. This bright, well-equipped hostel offers family rooms (£52) and bunks (£15), and if you wild camp outside will charge only £3 for its toilet and shower facilities. This is also the place to come to arrange sea kayaking with **Clearwater Paddling**.

Self-catering
There are many options on Barra, as well as the Visit Hebrides website (see page 58), check out www.isleofbarra.com.

Camping
For some reason, the local powers that be seem to have ignored the needs of campers on Barra so you'll need to wild camp. The machair by the airport (not the runway) at Traigh Mhor and Borve Point (west Barra) are popular. To ensure you don't risk the wrath of the crofters ensure all waste and litter is removed when you leave the site. For provisions, there are 2 well-stocked mini-supermarkets in Castlebay.

Vatersay p89
Self-catering
Those who find Barra too busy can escape to the silence and golden sands of neighbouring Vatersay.
Vatersay School, Mrs Patricia Barron, T/F01871-810283, www.vatersayschool. co.uk. A converted schoolhouse overlooking a glorious south-facing beach. It sleeps 6 and costs £575-850 per week.

🍴 Eating

A number of additional eating options can be found under Sleeping, above.

Berneray p83
♥♥-♥ **Lobster Pot**, Berneray, T01876-540288. Wed-Mon 0900-1700, Tue 0900-2000. Aside from a packed grocery shop (they'll deliver to the **Gatliff Trust Hostel**), there is a friendly

café (the only on the island) where you can tuck into toasties, crayfish salads, Salar salmon and home-baking.

Benbecula *p84*
¶¶¶-¶¶ The Stepping Stone Restaurant, Balivanich, T01870-603377. The best place to eat on Benbecula, with family links to the acclaimed MacLeans Bakery (of Hebridean Oatcake fame), half a mile up the road. Lunch-time specials may include cockles in oatmeal whilst in the Sinteas restaurant dinner (from 1800-2130) includes the likes of local lamb and dessert of traditional Crowdie and cream. 3 course set Sun lunch (£15).

South Uist *p85*
¶¶¶-¶¶ Orasay Inn, in the northeast, Lochcarnan. Isobel, the owner/chef, is a 'Natural Cooking of Scotland' trainer. Expect fresh and locally sourced game, lamb, beef, shellfish and vegetables, as well as freshly baked breads, scones and home-made desserts. The dining is relaxed, the service attentive and expect a warm welcome. Recommended.
¶¶¶-¶¶ Polochar Inn, see Sleeping, above. Good range of lunch and dinner options, with an emphasis on locally sourced produce. Try the hearty cullen skink (seafood) soup, the flakey smoked salmon with mussels or the leg of Uist lamb. Rustic interior with attentive service. Terrific food.

Eriskay *p87*
¶¶-¶ Am Politician, Baile, see page 87. This pub serves food (1200-2100), and occasionally hosts live bands. Its small conservatory offers lovely views over the sea.

Barra *p87*
¶¶¶-¶¶ Castlebay Hotel, Castlebay, T01871-810223, www.castlebayhotel.com. Overlooking Kisimul Castle and offering excellent fish and seafood.
¶¶¶-¶¶ Isle of Barra Hotel, Tangasdale Beach, T01871-810383, www.isleofbarrahotel.co.uk. Family-run hotel with an evening seafood restaurant and à la carte dining.

¶¶ Café Kisimul, on the main street, Castlebay, T01871-810645, www.cafekisimul.co.uk. The place to feast on tasty Italian and Indian fare with a seafood twist.
¶¶-¶ The Deck and Hebridean Toffee Shop, on the main street, Castlebay T01871-810898. Open Mar, Apr and May Mon-Sat 1000-1700, Jun-Aug Mon-Sat 1000-1800, Sun 1200-1700. Produces 1st-class toffee and will serve you tea, sandwiches and great home-baking on its deck overlooking the castle.
¶ The Otter Café, clearly signposted, by the Ardmhar ferry terminal, T01871-890269. Open daily. A great tea room and you can catch the ferry to Eriskay nearby.

⚙ Activities and tours

North Uist *p82*
Uist Outdoor Centre, Cearn Dusgaidh, Lochmaddy, T01876-500480, www.uistoutdoorcentre.co.uk. Runs week-long kayaking courses as well as weekend beginners' trips; scuba-diving; rock climbing and abseiling from sea cliffs; survival courses; and power-boat courses. For those wishing for even more solitude there are overnight expeditions to Pabbay and Boreray, where you can see dolphins, porpoises, minke whales, grey seals and basking sharks. You can also charter an RIB for a trip to St Kilda (38 nautical miles west), the Shiants, Monach and Flannan Islands. The centre provides accommodation (see Sleeping, page 90).

South Uist *p85*
Golf
Askernish Golf Club, Lochboisdale, South Uist, T01878-700083, www.askernishgolfclub.com. Recently 'rediscovered' amidst the machair, this may soon be promoted far and wide as one of the world's classic links courses, having been laid out in 1891 by the legendary Scottish golfer, 'Old Tom Morris.'

Barra *p87*
Boat trips
Barra Fishing Charters, Northbay, T01871-890384, www.barrafishingcharters.com. Run

by local fisherman Donald MacLeod, who offers a range of trips aboard his 10-m-long cruiser, *Boy James*. Fishing enthusiasts (free tackle and rods) pay £40 for a 4-hr offshore trip. Those who wish to take to the high seas without fishing kit can instead explore the remote but spectacular Hebridean isle of Mingulay from £50 per person (£25 per child). This 6-hr trip includes a 2-hr sail from Barra past the neighbouring islands of Sandray and Pabbay, a circumnavigation of Mingulay to view the spectacularly high western sea cliffs, and a landing on the east coast for a 3-hr exploration of the beautiful beach of Mingulay Bay, the deserted village and surrounding hills and coast. There are also fine views to the lighthouse on Barra Head, the most southerly outpost of the Outer Hebrides island chain where, weather permitting, the *Boy James* will also sail. It's also possible to charter the boat for private hire or wildlife excursions – call for prices.

Kayaking
Clearwater Paddling, just along from the Co-op and **Heritage Museum**, Dunard, Castlebay, T01871-810443, www.clearwater paddling.com. Experienced operator that offers a range of half-day (£30), full-day (£60) and week-long sea-kayaking trips from Barra. Also run the **Dunard Hostel** in Castlebay.

Taxi tours
Campbell Taxis, T01871-810216; and Lochmaddy, T01876-500215, for island tours.

⊖ Transport

For information on local bus journeys, see Getting around, page 81.

Berneray *p83*
Ferry From **Berneray** to **Harris**, 3-4 times daily, 1 hr. A one-way ticket costs £6.50 per passenger, £29.50 per car.

Benbecula *p84*
Air Flybe/Loganair flies to **Glasgow** from **Benbecula**, Mon-Sat, twice daily, 1 hr. There are also flights from **Benbecula** to **Barra**, Mon-Fri 1 daily, 20 mins.
Car hire Ask Car Hire, Linicleit, T01870-602818 www.askcarhire.com; **Maclennan Bros Ltd**, Balivanich, T01870-602191.

South Uist *p85*
Car hire Laing Motors, Lochboisdale, T01870-700267, www.laingmotors.co.uk.
Cycle hire Rothan Cycles, by the Gatliff Trust Hostel, 9 Howmore, T01870-620283, www.rothan.com. Hires basic bikes for £10 and tourers for £12. It's £18 and £20 respectively for 2 days. Will also repair your bike and deliver to/pick-up at Eriskay (£20), Lochboisdale (£15) and Berneray (£28).
Ferry No boats leave South Uist on Sun. **Lochboisdale** to **Oban**, 1 daily, Tue, Thu and Sat, 5 hrs 20 mins and via **Castlebay** (Barra) on Sun, 6 hrs 30 mins.

Barra *p87*
Air Flybe/Loganair flies to **Glasgow** from Barra, 1 daily, Mon-Sat, 1 hr 5 mins.
Car hire Barra Car Hire, Hugh MacNeil, Northbay, T01871-890313. **Barra Cycle Hire**, 29 St Brendans Rd, Castle- bay, T01871-810284. Hires bikes (starting from £10), booking recommended.
Ferry Castlebay to **Oban**, Mon, Wed, Fri, Sat, Sun, 4 hrs 50 mins. Also sailings via **Lochboisdale** on Tue and Thu, 7 hrs 20 mins. There is also a sailing via **Coll** and **Tiree**, Thu, 6 hrs 45 mins. To **Tiree**, £7.35 per passenger, £36.50 per car. Ferry from **Castlebay** to **Lochboisdale**, Tue and Thu, £6.70 per passenger, £19.55 per car.

There are also early morning departures to **Lochboisdale**, Wed and Fri, 0700, Sun 2050. Ferries sail from Barra to **Eriskay** at least 3 times daily. A one-way ticket costs £7 per passenger and £20.30 per car, a 5-day return is £11.85 per passenger and £35.50 per car. Bikes are free.

St Kilda

Forty one miles west of the Outer Hebrides lie the spectacular and isolated islands of St Kilda, Scotland's first UNESCO World Heritage Site and home to the largest colony of seabirds in northern Europe. St Kilda consists of several islands, remnants of an ancient volcano, and manages to capture the imagination of most visitors to the Outer Hebrides, whether they actually get there or just dream about romantic voyages to mysterious lands across perilous seas. Inhabited for almost 4000 years until evacuated by its remaining 36 islanders on 29 August 1930, the isles which are also a National Nature Reserve were bequeathed to the National Trust for Scotland in 1957. Each year, during the brief summer months teams of volunteers work on Hirta, maintaining what remains of the abandoned houses, studying the wildlife and glorying in the peace and isolation of a dramatic island group inhabited by a million seabirds and where the Soay sheep has bred for thousands of years.

Ins and outs

A 14-hour boat journey from Oban and eight hours from the Outer Hebrides, St Kilda is a long way out in the North Atlantic. The cost and the sea conditions are the two factors that will make or break your plans to reach St Kilda, but from expert sea kayakers on an expedition, to yachts and cruise boats, it is possible … at a price. **Island Cruising** ① *1 Erista, Uig, Lewis, T01851-672381, www.island-cruising.com*, arranges boat trips to St Kilda from April to October starting from £580 (four-day all-inclusive). The tour comprises the journey to and from St Kilda and a landing on Hirta with a visit to the museum, the old village and a wider exploration of the island, including a climb up to the highest sea cliffs in the British Isles at Conachair (430 m). They also run a six-day cruise (£795) allowing an extra day or two on St Kilda and will often try to visit the isolated, wildlife rich isles of the Monach's and North Rona en route. **Seatrek** ① *16 Uigean, Uig, Lewis, T01851-672469, www.seatrek. co.uk*, run day trips to St Kilda, departing at 0730 with three to four hours spent ashore (weather and tides permitting) before returning for 1900. The cost is £180 per person. **Uist Outdoor Centre** ① *North Uist, T01876-500480, www.uistoutdoorcentre.co.uk*, say their 1½-hour power- boat trip to St Kilda is the fastest way to get there. For trips to St Kilda, see www.outdoor hebrides.com, and the 'Visiting St Kilda' portal at www.nts.org.uk.

   National Trust for Scotland ① *www.nts.org.uk, T0844-493 2237*, also organizes fortnight long voluntary work parties in the summer months every year to undertake restoration,

How St Kilda was killed off

Friday 29 August 1930 was the end of life as it had been for centuries on St Kilda. For a least 1000 years the inhabitants of this remote group of islands had been tenants of the Macleods of Dunvegan on Skye. In earlier days the trip from Skye, undertaken in longboats, would require 16 hours of rigorous rowing and sailing. Even now, the trip to St Kilda is no easy matter.

Until 1930 the islanders had been supported from the mainland by the provision of a nurse and a post office. But the Scottish Office decided that their subsidy of the islands was no longer economic. This meant that life for the residents without those facilities would be untenable.

In 1930, to the younger of the 36 residents, including a man with nine children, evacuation was an attractive prospect. There would be better schooling for the children, and better health care. Although many had never seen a tree, a new life in forestry appealed. The more elderly residents, most of whom had never left the island and who could not speak English, must have viewed the drastic change with alarm but the younger majority view prevailed and evacuation was planned.

There were 500 Soay sheep to be moved first. Their coats of fine wool were not sheared but plucked by the inhabitants using only a penknife. The resultant locally woven tweed, either shipped ashore or sold to rare visitors, had provided the inhabitants' only contact with actual money. No taxes on income or on anything else were paid. Their internal economy took the form of barter. The plentiful supply of gannets, when dried, provided winter food. No inhabitant had ever fought in any war. Their distance and isolation earned them no consideration by the rest of Scotland.

Despite protestations by the Canine Defence League, all dogs were destroyed. Just two were put down by injections of hydrocyanic acid. The rest, at the islanders' insistence, had stones tied around their necks and were hurled from the jetty. Small boats were used to ferry only a dozen or so sheep out to the SS Dunara Castle. Ten cows with four calves were also evacuated. Then HMS Harebell, of the Fishery Protection Service, came on the final day to take the islanders to the mainland. The Under Secretary of State for Scotland imposed a ban on photography, thus ensuring the people of St Kilda privacy during the evacuation. It was not possible to house all of the inhabitants in Argyll, as had been hoped, so the community was split, their communal lives coming to an end.

The history of the island has been documented in a number of scholarly works, including *The Life and Death of St Kilda* by Tom Steel, and *Island on the Edge of the World* by Charles Maclean.

maintenance and archaeology projects around the old village on Hirta. The groups are very popular and each volunteer must complete an application form, so apply early. The fortnight costs over £750 per person and this covers transport from Oban to St Kilda and all food and basic lodging costs while on the island. Note that the sea journey can be arduous.

Sights

In 1957 the islands become the property of the National Trust for Scotland, and in 1986 a UNESCO World Heritage Site. St Kilda is the most important seabird breeding station in northwest Europe. The islands are home to a quarter of the world's population of northern gannets, the largest colony of fulmars in Britain and one of the largest colonies of puffins in Scotland. These huge numbers of seabirds were vital to the islanders' survival. Their eggs provided food in the summer, and gannets and fulmers were caught each season to be plucked, dried and stored for the winter. Their feathers and oil were kept for export, whilst their bones were shaped into useful tools and their skins into shoes.

The largest of the islands, **Hirta**, was the remotest community in Britain, if not Europe, until 1930, when the remaining 36 Gaelic-speaking inhabitants were evacuated at their own request, in one of the most poignant episodes of Scottish history (see box, page 96). Today, Hirta is partly occupied by the army as a radar-tracking station for the rocket range on South Uist and managed by Scottish Natural Heritage. Across a narrow channel lies **Dun**. Nearby **Boreray** is home to the world's largest colony of gannets, and **Soay** on which the rare Soay sheep breed, completes the group. There are several dramatic 'stacs' rising sheer from the Atlantic Ocean. At 430 m, the sea cliffs at Conachair are the highest in the British Isles.

Contents

Footnotes

Index